A TREASURY OF NEEDLEWORK DESIGNS

March Comes In Like A Lion sampler worked by Martha R. Zimiles. Design, pages 196–97.

A TREASURY OF NEEDLEWORK DESIGNS

Martha Rogers Zimiles

VAN NOSTRAND REINHOLD COMPANY
New York Cincinnati Toronto London Melbourne

Acknowledgments

I would like to thank all my friends who gave me so much of their time preparing the samples for this book. In alphabetical order, thank you: Mary Ann Anderson, Harriett Bates, Ruth Foster, Janice Gablemann, Sharon Hiltz, Jane Kennedy, Martha Kennedy, Gladys Reynolds, Floey Russell, Joan Strathdee, Fessenden Wilder, and Merrill Wilder. Special thanks go to my long-suffering husband Murray who took the photographs.

This book is dedicated to my friends at The Designing Woman Shop, Lakeville, Connecticut
Harriette Fearing, Helen Hartcorn, Jinny Palmer and Anita Westsmith
with thanks for all they have taught me

Copyright © 1976 by Litton Educational Publishing, Inc.

Library of Congress Catalog Card Number 76-11452
ISBN 0-442-29584-7   (paper)

All rights reserved.
Printed in the U.S.A.

Published in 1976 by Van Nostrand Reinhold Company
A Division of Litton Educational Publishing, Inc.
450 West 33rd Street
New York, NY 10001, U.S.A.

Van Nostrand Reinhold Limited
1410 Birchmount Road
Scarborough, Ontario M1P 2E7, Canada

Van Nostrand Reinhold Australia Pty. Ltd.
17 Queen Street
Mitcham, Victoria 3132, Australia

Van Nostrand Reinhold Company Ltd.
Molly Millars Lane
Wokingham, Berkshire, England

16 15 14 13 12 11 10 9 8 7 6 5 4 3 2

Library of Congress Cataloging in Publication Data

Zimiles, Martha.
  A treasury of needlework designs.

  Includes index.
  1. Needlework—Patterns. 2. Embroidery—
Patterns.
I. Title.
TT753.Z55   746.4'4   76-11452
ISBN 0-442-29584-7

Contents

How To Use This Book 6

Materials and Procedure for Needlepoint 7

Materials and Procedure for Embroidery 11

Flowers and Leaves 12

Birds 54

Animals 70

Insects 98

Sea Creatures 102

Fruits, Vegetables, and Kitchen Motifs 108

Transportation 118

Religious Subjects and Holidays 132

Heraldry 150

Sports and Hobbies 160

Country Life 168

Miscellaneous Projects 172

Alphabets 182

Borders 186

Samplers 188

Samples 198

Index of Designs 207

How To Use This Book

This is not another "how to" book. It is a workbook for those needleworkers, experienced and beginners alike, who would like to create something original but do not trust their own drawing ability. Here is a sourcebook of more than 350 designs of different sizes and degrees of complexity, in a variety of styles, with countless uses and infinite possibilities for choices of color, shading, pattern, and ornamental stitches.

These drawings provide a starting point, an armature on which to build up one's own creation. Here is a way for the needleworker to use as little or as much imagination as she or he has, to make an original! Here is a way to produce a much more personal piece of work than can ever be provided by a mail-order kit. It is also a way to avoid the paint-by-the-numbers philosophy of even the handsomest hand-painted canvas bought in a store. Finally, there is all the excitement of choosing one's own wool, colors, stitches, not to mention the great saving that can be made with this expensive pastime by investing in basic supplies and working from scratch.

When your work is completed it will be one of a kind, because no two people starting with the same drawing will select exactly the same colors, stitches, tonalities, and way of using the lines and flat spaces.

Although the designs in this book were planned for needlepoint and embroidery, they can of course be used by many kinds of craftsmen. For example, they can be adapted for rug hooking, leather tooling, tapestry weaving, découpage, and even wood appliqué.

Don't be afraid to really use this workbook. It has been designed so that the pages can be easily removed to be used and then saved in a three-ring loose-leaf. If you have a positive aversion to removing pages from a book, it is always possible to trace the design you select onto another sheet of paper. Those with no qualms can color right on the page or write in stitch indications.

Although the designs are in black and white and consist primarily of lines—think color! A black line can be treated as an outline in a piece of needlework, but it can also and equally effectively indicate the point at which two areas of color meet.

Solid black areas or areas shaded with dots are intended only to make an appealing drawing and help distinguish one area from another. It does not mean that black or a dark color yarn is indicated in that space.

Some of the drawings are for large projects. The drawing may go right to the edge of the book page. In such cases it is useful to remember to cut a generous margin of canvas so the design won't be crowded. Pillows and other stuffed items are rounded when complete, and ample background will give a design some elbow room.

Some of the designs use more than one book page. All parts of a design should be removed or traced, interfering margins trimmed and the whole matched up, pieced together with tape, and laid flat before any drawing or painting on canvas is done.

Some designs are small or are single motifs with no special indications for use. These can be used singly, on small projects, such as a tie, headband, checkbook cover, belt, pocket, appliqué for a handbag, TV Guide cover, eyeglass case, cases for contact lenses or jewelry, purse, cosmetics kit, tobacco pouch, or for any other projects one can dream up. The motifs can also be used in groups or repeats on larger projects such as tote bags, racquet covers, telephone book covers, TV covers, chair seats, stool covers, piano benches, rugs, wall hangings, banners, pictures, card-table covers, pillows, ottomans, and so on.

Some of the designs were conceived with specific projects in mind, but indications for these (the handbag outlines and fold marks, for example) can be disregarded if another use is desired.

With each drawing or group of related motifs is a note of the most suitable canvas mesh size (see discussion of materials below for description). You can always choose a finer mesh than indicated, but if you use coarser canvas, it is recommended that you eliminate some details from the design.

The usefulness of this book can be greatly increased by realizing the freedom to adapt details from some of the larger designs for single or repeat use on smaller items.

You are not even strictly bound to the size of the drawing as it appears in this book. If an item is preferred larger or smaller it does not have to be redrawn. It can be enlarged or reduced photographically by the photostat process at a very small cost. (Consult the Yellow Pages under Photo Copying.)

In some instances suggestions are given for ornamental needlepoint stitches. This is not to say that fancy stitches must be used or that others cannot be substituted. These are only suggestions, not rules.

Most designs are improved by a good border, and you may wish to make up your own. Often one works wonders by simply using bands of different colors in different widths around the design. Some drawings show margins for borders. Included in this book are drawings for borders with a motif. There are also some samples of borders made from a combination of ornamental stitches.

When using any border other than plain bands of color in tent stitch, it is best to lay out or count out the border first. Then correct canvas dimensions can be determined and the design can be centered perfectly within the border.

Many people like to monogram and even date their work, much to the delight of future collectors. For that purpose two alphabets, block and fancy, are shown on graphs. One set of numbers is provided. The graphs reproduce the 14 mesh per inch and 12 mesh per inch of the most common canvas sizes. The graphs can be counted onto any size canvas but the size of the letter or number will be relative to the mesh size used.

Materials and Procedure for Needlepoint

There are certain basic materials one needs and others that it is useful to be familiar with before beginning. But there is one thing to remember—always use good-quality materials. This is only showing a proper respect for your own time and effort. After all, needlepoint and embroidery are time-consuming crafts. The hope is to create an object of enduring beauty and usefulness, perhaps even an heirloom. It is time and effort wasted to put hours of work into sleazy materials.

The basics of needlepoint are canvas and yarn.

Canvas comes in three different types. The oldest is called penelope and is distinguished by its double weave of warp and weft threads that form a pattern of open weave. This may be a little confusing to the eye at first. The pairs of threads can be separated to create a mesh for petit-point stitches, and the canvas is often used this way for a detail within a larger whole. Penelope canvas usually comes in a brown or écru color which does not make it the most suitable ground for painting.

Mono canvas comes in both écru and white and is a single, plain weave. It is easier on the eyes, and the white gives true and bright colors when painted. The single weave is somewhat less stable then penelope; if you work too tightly, mono canvas will tend to distort, although blocking should overcome this problem in most cases. A few of the fancy stitches work up less well on mono canvas, and a small number cannot be done on mono at all.

Interlock canvas is a relative newcomer. As quality improves, it will probably become more and more popular. It is also a double-woven mesh, but the pairs of threads are very close together, giving the appearance of mono. It also comes in white and has the advantage of distorting less than mono. However, I have not found any brand that is completely satisfactory. Perhaps because of the type of weave or the amount of sizing, interlock can be harsh on wool and cause it to either fuzz or wear thin.

Canvas comes in several sizes. The size number refers to the number of mesh per running inch. The mesh is the crossing of a horizontal and a vertical (a warp and a weft) thread. That little crossing is the basic needlepoint unit, the area covered by one tent stitch. The more mesh there are per inch, the finer the canvas and the smaller the individual stitch. Number 10 is rather coarse and is especially good for rugs and large items or designs without too much detail. Numbers 12, 13, and 14 are medium sizes. Needlepoint done on number 18 and smaller sizes is referred to as petit point and requires good eyesight and in some cases a magnifier to work comfortably. Numbers 5 and 7 are used for rugs and quickpoint, and the larger designs in this book are suitable for these.

There are several manufacturers of canvas, both foreign and domestic. Select material with strong, even threads, free from knots, lumps, thin spots, or breaks, and not overly slick or stiff with sizing.

Many brands of yarn, covering all degrees of quality, are available. For needlepoint there are two basic types of wool. Tapestry yarn, which is tightly spun four-ply and should not be separated, is suitable for 12–14 canvas. Persian yarn, however, is the finest wool for needlepoint. It is more adaptable to different canvas sizes because it is composed of three separately spun plies which can be used singly or together to suit the canvas size. Good quality Persian yarns come in a fabulous array of colors.

Other fibers can be used, either by themselves or as points of contrast in a wool project. There are cotton and linen embroidery floss, beautiful silks, metal and ecclesiastical threads, as well as a variety of synthetics.

Needles for needlepoint are referred to as tapestry needles and come in various sizes. They all must have a blunt point and a long eye.

There is quite a range in what one need spend on materials used in transferring the designs in this book to needlepoint canvas. The one invariable rule is to use good quality.

I believe that it is worth the extra investment in materials and preparation time to do a fairly complete job of transferring the design and working out the colors before you stitch. Much depends on the complexity of the design. Less complex ones can be simply traced onto the canvas with an indelible (always indelible) marker in gray or black. Many people want to have nothing to do with paints. In that case markers, crayons, or colored pencils can be used to work out the color scheme in coloring-book fashion right on the page (but never on the canvas), which then becomes a reference chart to aid in putting the wool colors in the right places. If you do not paint the canvas and the colors of the wools are to be darker shades, it is a good idea to use a black indelible marker on écru canvas. This way the bits of canvas that sometimes show through will not be obvious.

If the outline drawing is done on white canvas because most of the colors are light, but the background wool is dark, paint in the background first.

For complex designs with many colors or a lot of shading, it is advisable to apply color directly to the canvas. In the long run this saves time and avoids the frustration of continual decision making. Lines and shapes and shading proceed more smoothly. The color provides a foundation under the wool in the event of disaster (moths, burns) or wear so that the canvas does not show through in an obvious way. It is always a good idea to paint in the background where a dark color wool is used to avoid a sort of bald or sparse look where the canvas shows through.

You can avoid painting but still use some color by investing in colored marking pens. As with all needlepoint materials, they must be completely waterproof. I know of only one brand made specifically for needlepoint: Nepo markers come in a set of five basic colors and black. There are other brands which claim to be indelible but it is wise to test them in water and with any protective fabric spray (such as Scotch Gard) that is to be used on the finished piece.

The major limitation of marking pens is that the color range is limited and colors can't be mixed to conform accurately to the wools. For this reason marking pens, if used as the sole coloring agent, are not really useful in preparing canvases for sale. They do not make a beautiful or subtle painting.

That comes only with brushes and paint. There is no reason to be frightened at the prospect of wielding a brush and mixing colors. It is nowhere near as difficult as many people think.

Both oil paints and water-based plastic paints—acrylics—are used for needlepoint. Acrylics have the distinct advantage of mixing with water, thus minimizing the consequences of spilled paint and turpentine. They wash out of clothing easily before they set but they are indelible when dry. Best of all, they dry quickly—allowing a canvas to be completed in one sitting.

A basic kit, oil or acrylic, would include the following tubes of color: alizarin crimson, ultramarine blue, cadmium yellow, burnt sienna, white, and black. A wider range would include: "thalo" blue, "thalo" green, cadmium orange, yellow ochre, and burnt umber. It is unlikely you will ever need more than these.

Although it is not essential, one of the polymer mediums (either gloss or matte) helps extend acrylic paints without making them too watery.

It is especially important to buy good brushes. Cheap brushes create a mess, lose their "spring" almost immediately, and don't hold a point.

To begin, have one flat brush in white bristle for painting large areas such as backgrounds; for lines and fine details, a good round sable hair brush size 2 or 3; and for general purposes, a larger round sable, size 4.

Even if you intend to use only paints to provide color, a black or gray indelible marker is needed for tracing the design onto canvas.

Add to these basic supplies a drawing board or table surface, masking tape, ruler, white palette (such as a paper plate), a container of clean water, and a few hours of time undisturbed by dogs, cats, children, or spouses.

To begin, select a design on the basis of your ability as well as taste. The more detailed the design, the more skill is required.

Remove the design from the book or trace it onto another sheet of paper in bold black lines. It is not essential to trace every dot and detail, only what you intend to use. Use a fairly substantial tracing or visualizing paper, not a flimsy tissue. If the design takes up more than one book page, remove (or trace) all the parts and line them up carefully. Trim any margins that obscure the design, and tape the sheets together. Secure the design to the drawing board with masking tape at the corners. Measure the design and include any additional background or border you wish. Measure and cut the canvas, leaving a generous margin of canvas beyond the stitching area. For small projects about one and a half inches is adequate; for larger ones, leave two or three inches.

Center the canvas over the drawing and secure at the corners (and sides, if the piece is large) with masking tape. The black lines of the drawing will show clearly through the canvas.

With a gray or black indelible marker, trace what you will use of the design directly onto the canvas.

The drawing may now be removed or, at the risk of getting a little paint on it, left in place.

Now mix your colors and begin to paint. A little experience will teach you how much paint it takes to cover a given area and how much water and medium will give the right consistency and brilliance.

Experience will also show whether you prefer to paint all the areas of one color at once or whether you get a better feeling for the whole by doing a little here, a little there in random manner. Remember that a really beautiful design can be created from a very limited number of colors and that these can be worked out right on the page, coloring-book fashion, before you touch the canvas.

Unless your design is very large—or if time is limited—it is a good idea to mix all the colors first. In that way they can all be adjusted to each other. If you have already selected the wools, the "agreement" of colors is already accomplished and the paints can be mixed in any order. However, it is not always practical to buy the wools before painting because it is difficult to estimate the right quantities. But you can work from either direction—painting first and buying wools to match or vice versa.

It is always helpful to have swatches or a wool card but these are not easily obtained. It is a good idea to save one strand of every color you use and make a little tassle out of it. That way a reference collection is built up.

While painting, be sure to let each color dry before applying another next to it. (This is where acrylic paints have such an advantage over oils.) Try to avoid blending one color right into another. This may look like a lovely painting, but remember that yarns are separate and unmixable so that even in an area that shades gradually from light to dark, the shades lie one next to the other and do not mix. If you paint with this in mind, stitching will be that much easier.

When you finish painting, or whenever you pause (even for ten minutes), wash those good brushes well and pat the hairs into place. Never leave them in water.

When the canvas is dry remove it from the board and bind the edges with tape to keep it from raveling.

Always keep the wools and canvas clean and neat as you work. It's a good idea to wash your hands before working with light wools.

Preparing a canvas for needlepoint: (1) the design traced on the canvas; (2) the design painted; (3) the dark background painted; (4) the finished case. The design is the carnation (see page 17). Worked by Martha R. Zimiles, Millerton, New York. The finished case is also shown, in color, on the cover.

Materials and Procedures for Embroidery

The word "crewel" refers to woolen yarn used for embroidery. The designs in this book can be worked in all sorts of yarns, cotton floss, linen, silk, metal, and synthetic threads.

Traditional crewel yarn is a long-fiber, two-ply yarn that comes in various thicknesses. The best wools are English and French. They are fine, smooth, even, and not stretchy. The colors are beautiful and come in great variety.

Since embroidery does not cover the entire surface of the ground, as needlepoint does, the fabric upon which it is worked becomes part of the design. All sorts of colors and textures can be used. Belgian linen and linen twill are popular and are highly suited to crewel. But you can work on almost any fabric that is not too flimsy and has a good even weave. Silk and velvet are exotic and difficult to work on, but very beautiful. I enjoy working with wool on wool, using an even-weave, medium-weight worsted.

Crewel needles come in varying lengths and are sharp-pointed.

The best embroidery is done on a hoop or frame. The choices range from simple hand-held hoops to large floor frames.

There are several ways to transfer these designs to fabric for embroidery.

If the fabric is smooth, without nap or fuzziness, dressmakers' carbon can be used. Work on a hard surface. Remove the design from the book or trace it as described above for needlepoint. Find and mark the center of the design and the center of the fabric. Secure the fabric to the board or table so that it will not slip. Center the design over the fabric and weight down the design, leaving a side free to slip the carbon in between the fabric and the design. Use a dark or a light carbon, depending on which will contrast with the color of the fabric. Carefully trace down the design with a sharp pencil, being sure not to dislodge the drawing.

A second method is more tedious but very accurate. Use a sharp point such as a hat pin, half a needle lodged in the eraser end of a pencil, or an etcher's needle. Place a pad of felt or an old towel on a hard surface. On top of the pad place the design and pierce holes through the design all along the lines of the drawing, keeping the holes fairly close and even.

When the entire design has been pricked, center it over the fabric and secure both well. With some powdered charcoal or carpenters' chalk on a blackboard eraser (or its equivalent), rub in a circular motion so that powder is deposited on the fabric through the holes. Practice with a scrap of fabric to get a feeling for how much powder and how much pressure to use.

When the whole design has been dusted, remove the design sheet and connect the dots with an indelible laundry marker (ball-point type) if permanence is desired. For a washable line, use a little gouache and a fine paint brush.

The pricked design can be saved and used over many times.

A third method involves the use of a transfer pencil, usually pink. These pencils are available in art-supply stores. Select a design and trace it onto substantial tracing paper. Turn this over and on the reverse side follow all the lines and marks with a well-sharpened transfer pencil.

Center this tracing, transfer-pencil-side down, and iron it onto the fabric. It is best to do a test piece first to determine the correct thickness of line and temperature of the iron. The transfer will not be as clear on a fuzzy material as it will on a linen or twill.

You can note the stitches and work out the colors on the book page. Colored pencils are ideal for this. When the design has been transferred by one of the above methods, choose your yarns, consult a good book of stitches, and go to work.

Flowers and Leaves

Vase of Flowers
After Matisse. Use bright colors: the vase, table, and background would look nice done in ornamental stitches. Canvas size 10–12

Circular Floral
Motif for a pillow. Make needlepoint area a circle at least 11½ inches in diameter. Canvas size 12

Flowers in a Row
Match up the three strips to make a bell pull or border.

Geometric Flower
Canvas size 10–14

15

Oranges and Orange Blossoms
Detail from the Unicorn Tapestries. To be richly shaded. Canvas size 14

Carnation
Little case that folds into an envelope.
Close with a snap. Sample, page 10 and
on the cover. Canvas size 14–18

Sunflowers
After William Morris. Makes a circular cushion, chair seat, or stool cover. Sample, page 198 and on the cover.
Canvas size 12–14

Pansies
Will fit into Sudberry House trays.
Also makes a nice border. Canvas
size 14

Floral Motifs
Use alone or in groups for purses, belts, little cases, coasters, luggage straps, bell pulls, etc. Canvas size 14–18

Bell Flowers
Eyeglass case if folded, sewn, and left open at one end. Multipurpose little case if open at the side. Canvas size 14–18

Daisy
One makes a coaster; line a row up on luggage straps. Canvas size 12–14

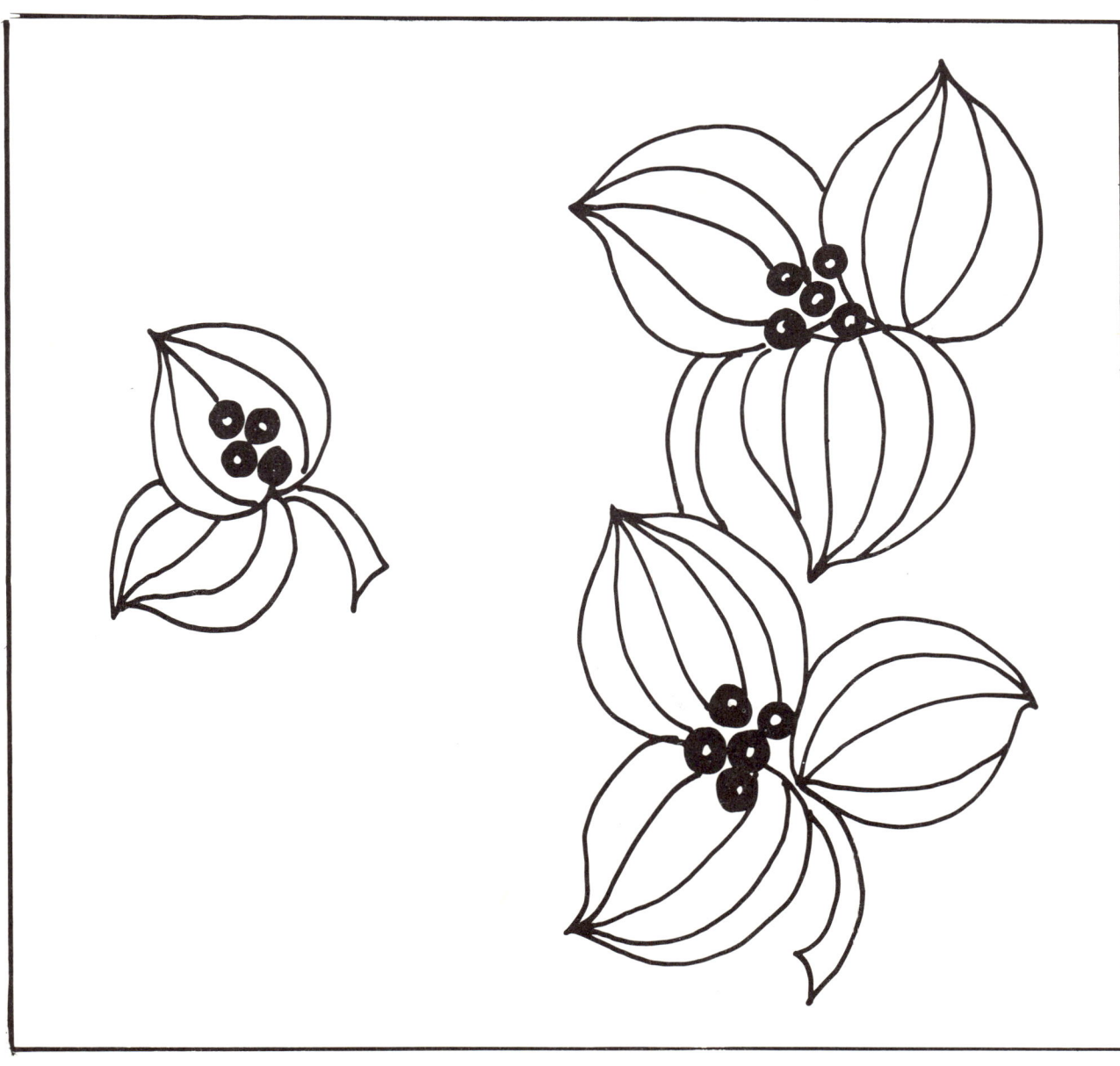

Maine Bunchberries
Eyeglass case if open at one end. Multipurpose little case if open at the side. Canvas size 14

Floral Motifs
Panels for handbag. Make a 2½-inch gusset to go around them. Sample, page 198 and on the cover. Canvas size 14

Jumble of Flowers
Fold in the middle for a checkbook cover or use for small pillow. Canvas size 14

Art Nouveau Rose
Pincushion, sachet, pocket, appliqué for handbag. Canvas size 14

Art Nouveau Flowers
For a Bermuda bag. Make two, or put an ornate monogram on the other side. The design is made to fit Sudberry House wooden bag handles; adjust outline to fit other handles. Sample on the cover. Canvas size 12–14

1880s Floral
After a tile by William Morris. Sample, page 199 and on the cover. Canvas size 12

Norwegian Floral
Design for a handbag. Make two and a gusset 3 to 5 inches wide to go between them, or, for professional mounting, choose a leather gusset. Canvas size 14

Petunias
Make square or round going in any direction. Canvas size 12–14

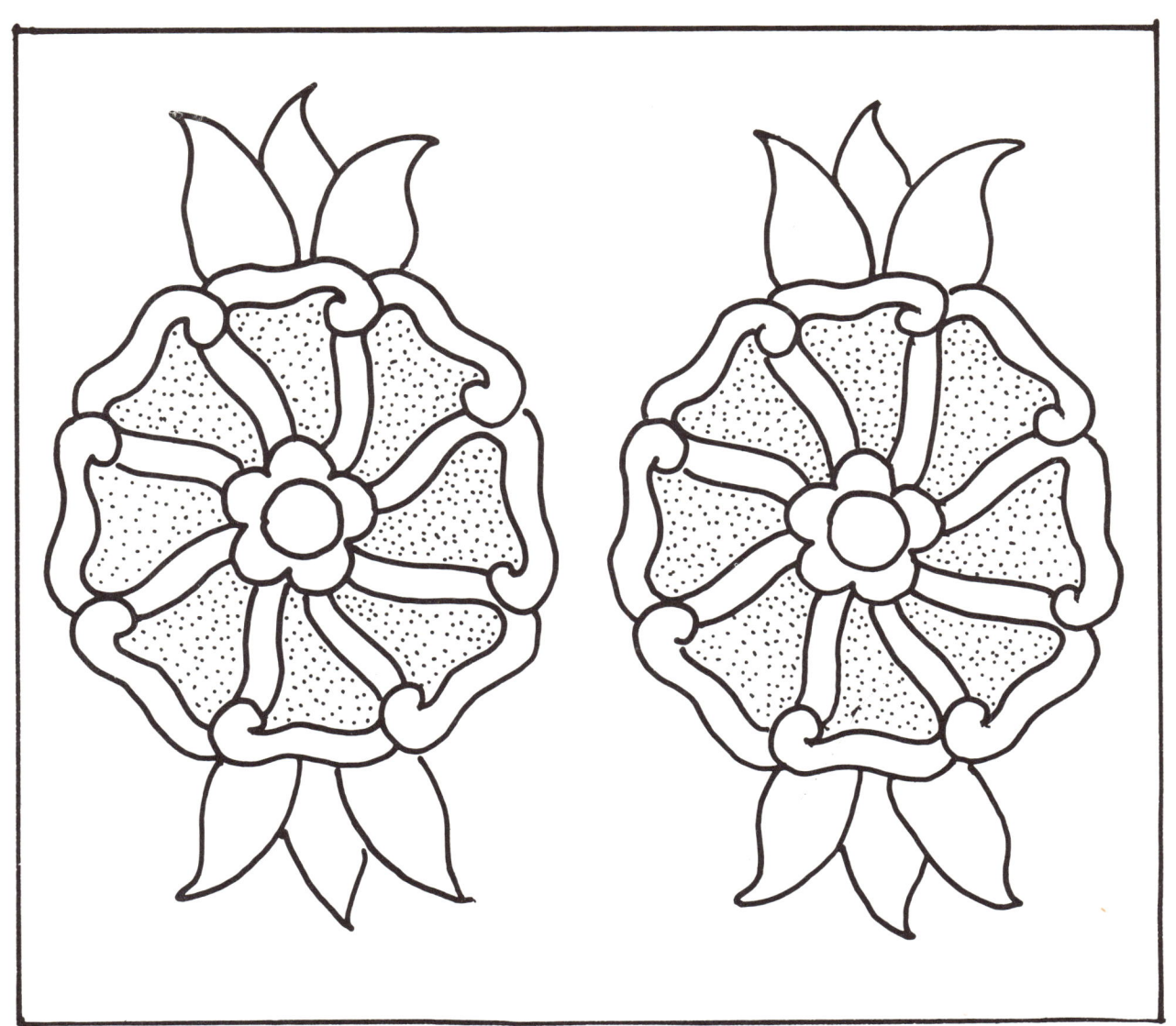

Chinese Flower
Small case for contact lenses, accesories, jewelry, cosmetics, etc. Make side closing with zipper or Velcro.
Canvas size 12–14

Wild Rose
An eyeglass case. Canvas size 14–18

Floral Motif
Luggage rack strap, bell pull or border. Canvas size 10–14

Sprig of Flowers
Detail from the background of French "millefleur" medieval tapestries. Canvas size 14–18

Basket of Flowers
Canvas size 18

Paisleys
Eyeglass or multipurpose case. Canvas size 14

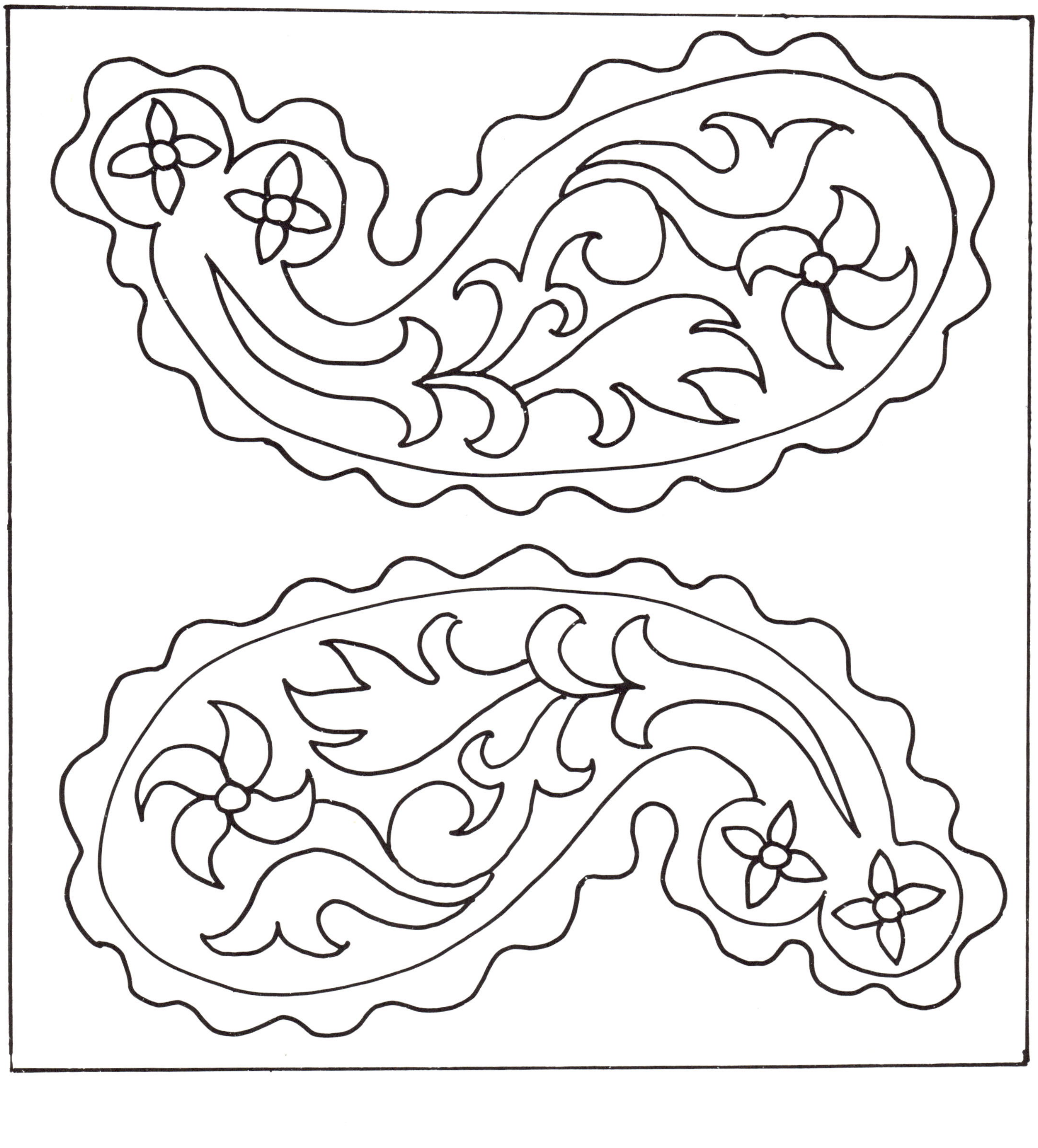

Wild Rose, pink with red hips

Wildflowers
This series consists of ten different designs. They are especially effective in crewel but can be done in needlepoint on number 14 canvas. Make individual crewel or needlepoint pillows, pictures, or chair seats. Combine them for a beautiful crewel bed cover: join them like a quilt with strips of fabric that contrast with the background. Or use some or all to make a needlepoint rug: put a border, even just a plain band of color, around each square and sew together (see instructions for tree-leaf rug on page 52).

Red Clover, purplish pink

Bindweed, pale blue

Columbine, red, yellow

Black-eyed Susans, dark brown with yellow petals, and white daisies with yellow centers

Trilliums, red, pink, and white

Vetch, purplish blue

Iris, blues, yellows

Dandelion, yellow flower would be amusing in Turkey tufting (either needlepoint or crewel)

Mountain Laurel, pale pink

Leaves
Use by themselves or as a group.
Canvas size 12–14

Scottish Thistle
Canvas size 14–18

Pine Cone and Needles
Canvas size 14–18

Maple Leaf
Do in a variety of bright fall colors or in summer greens. Canvas size 14

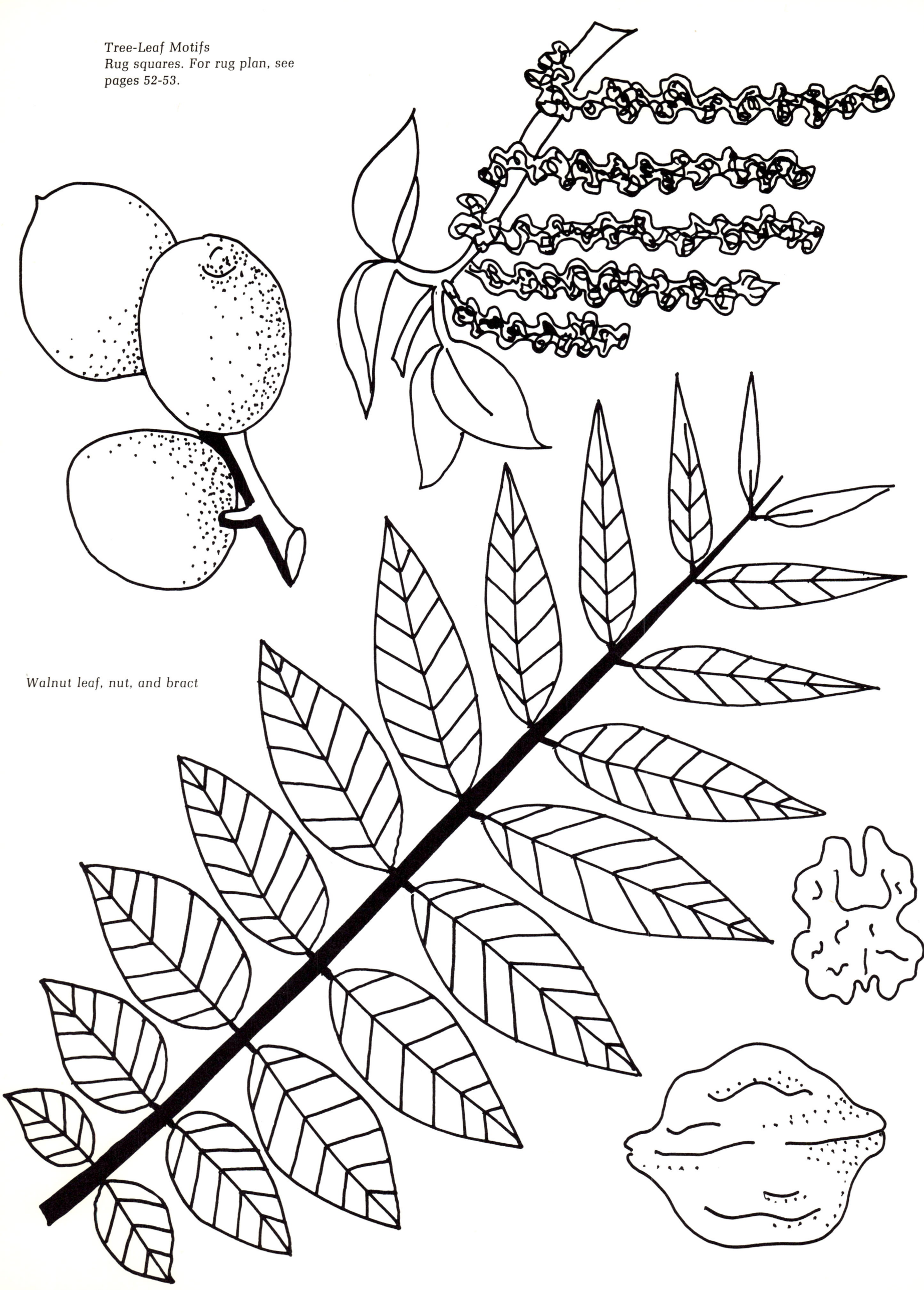

Tree-Leaf Motifs
Rug squares. For rug plan, see pages 52-53.

Walnut leaf, nut, and bract

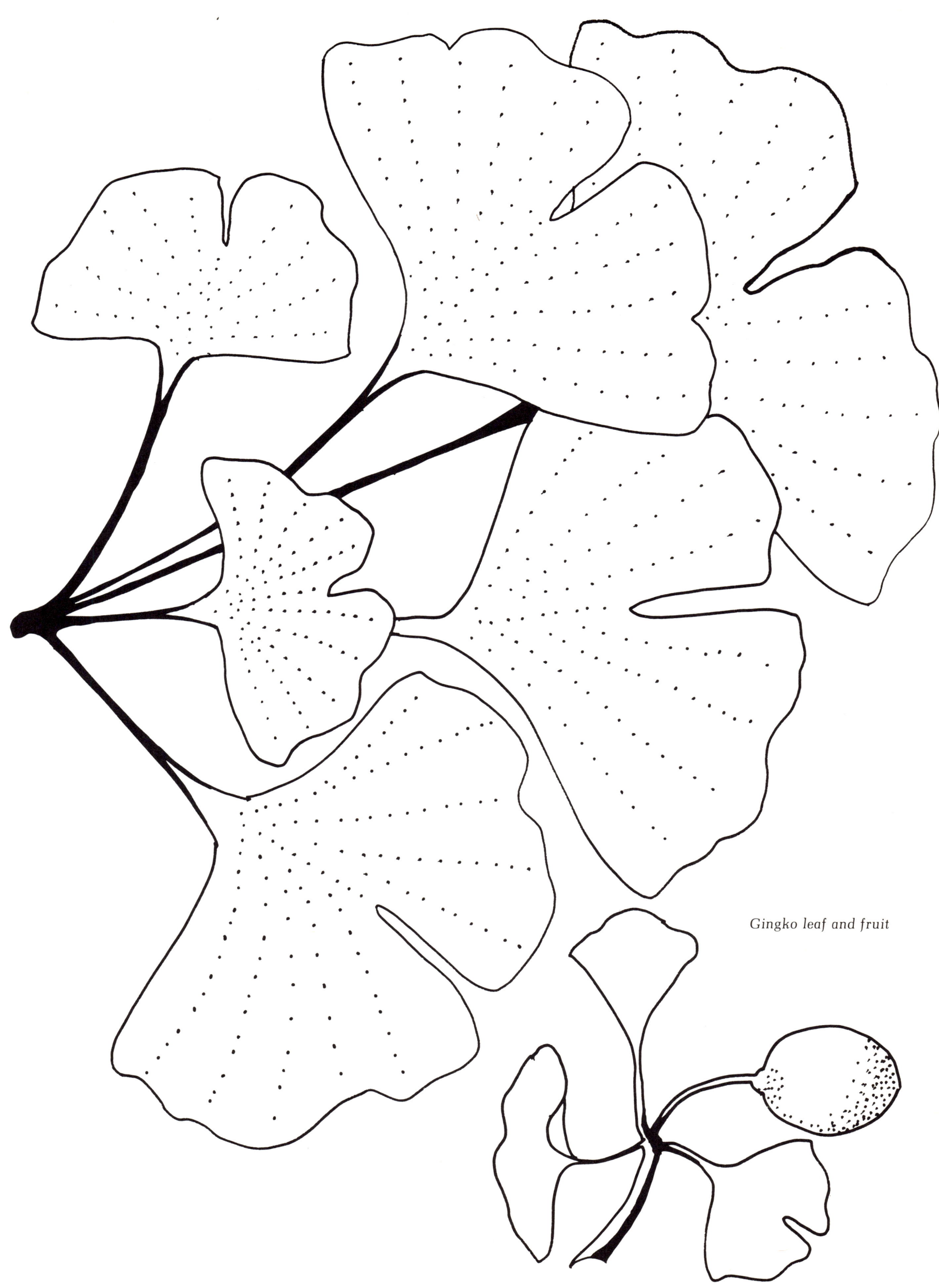

Gingko leaf and fruit

Maple leaf, blossom, and seed pod

Locust leaf, blossom, and seed pod

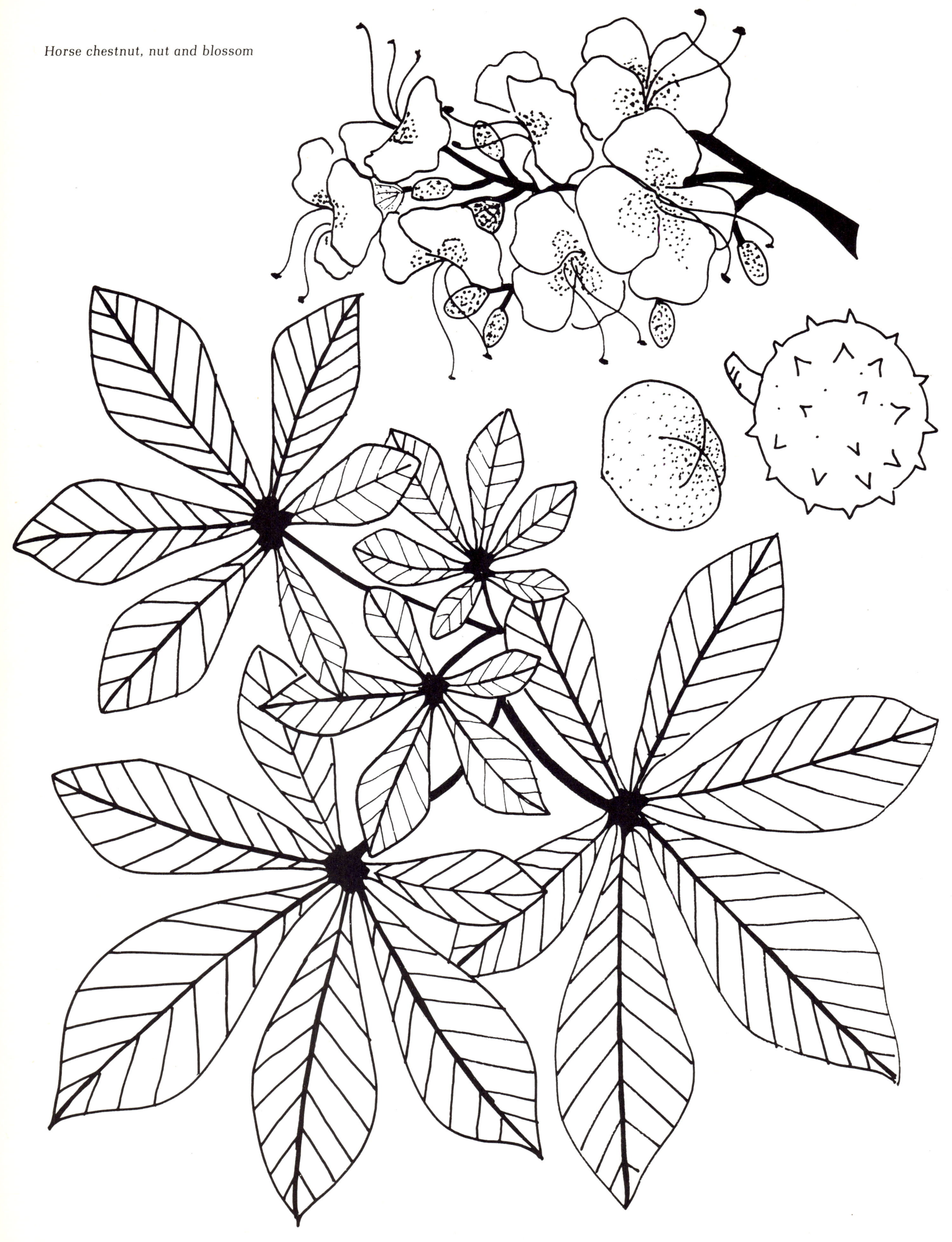
Horse chestnut, nut and blossom

Oak, acorn, and bract

Plan for Tree-Leaf Rug

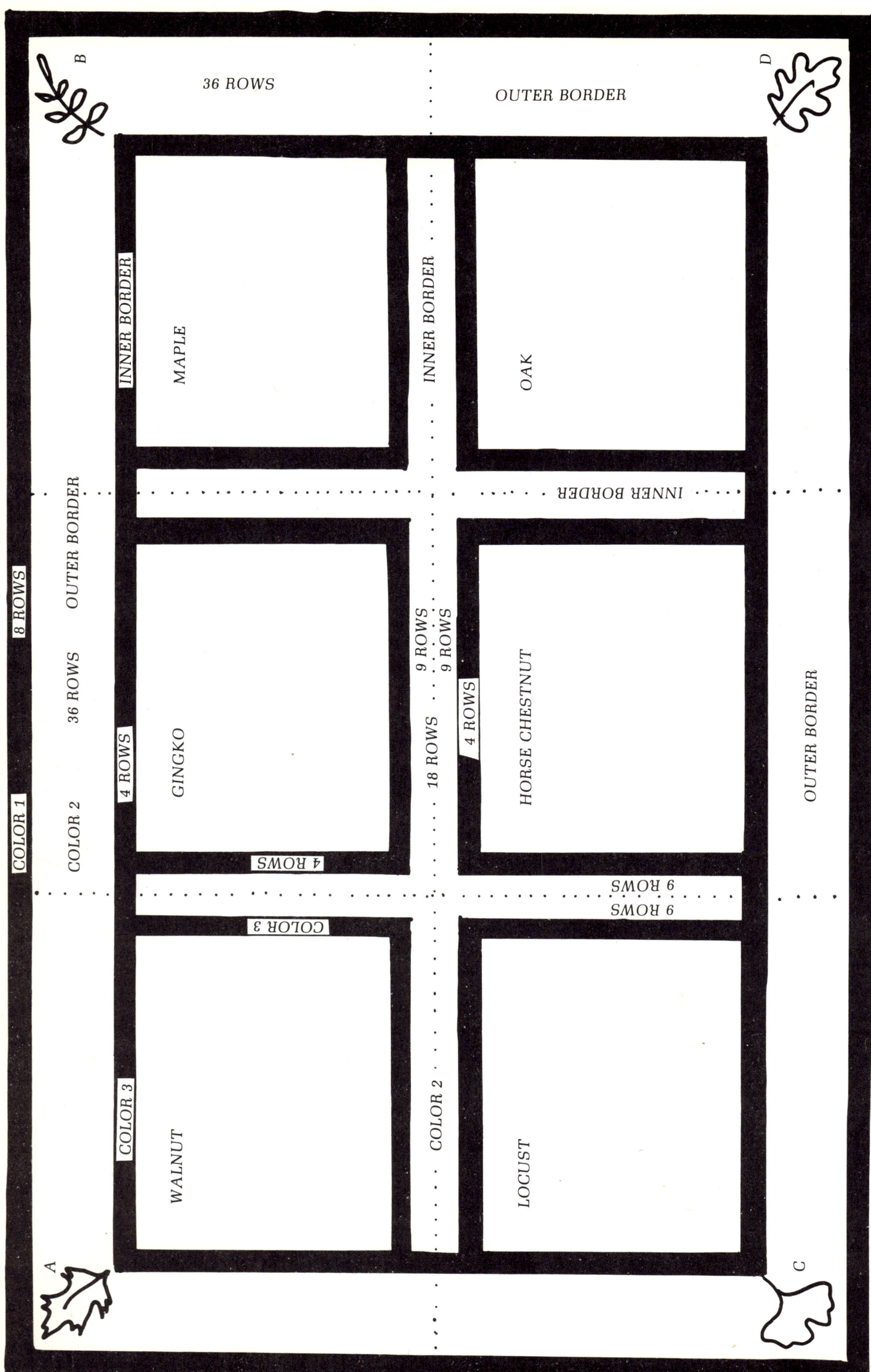

The six tree-leaf designs on pages 46–51 are good for needlepoint and crewel. The plan provided above is for a needlepoint rug, to be worked in separate sections or as one large canvas. The plan shows placement of each square and each corner motif. The dotted lines indicate how to do the rug in six sections. In this case, each square would include a section of the outer and inner borders that surround it. The numbers indicate the number of rows of stitches—counted in canvas threads, never holes. If the rug is done in sections, the border of eighteen rows of color 2 is divided in half, giving nine rows of color 2 on each section, as the diagram shows. Each square is labeled and each corner motif has a letter corresponding to the corner motifs shown opposite. The corner motifs can be traced onto the canvas but the border bands of color must be counted out in the number of canvas threads indicated by the numbers. The bands are drawn here only to show the positioning of the corner motifs.

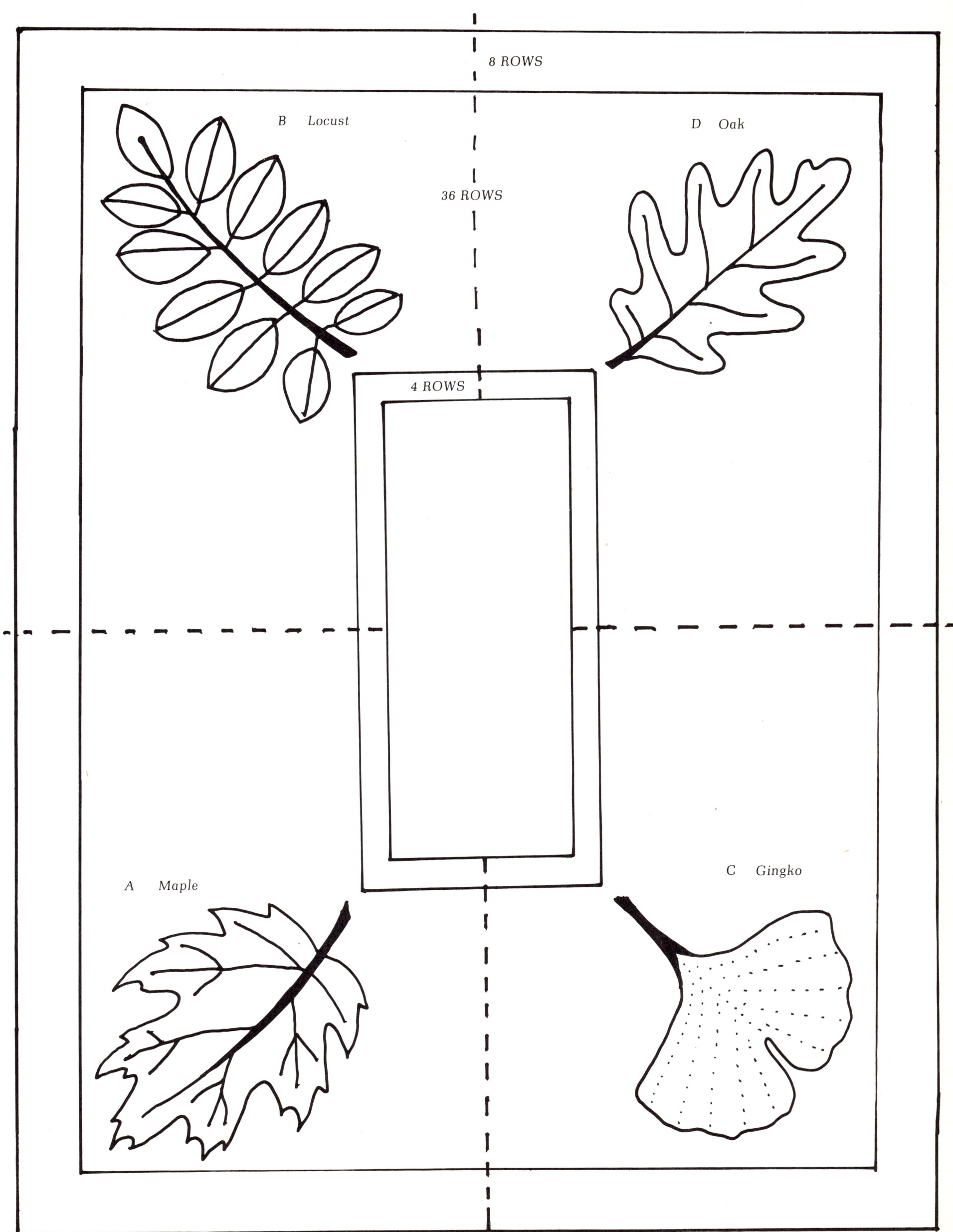

Birds

Chickadees

Robin

Bluebirds

Red-winged Blackbird

Birds
These would be nice coasters; four joined together with borders would make a pillow; while using all in a row would make a bell pull. Canvas size 14–18

Blue Jay

Goldfinch

Barn Swallow

Cardinal

Jungle Parrot
Bright colors go well here. Canvas size 14

Cardinals
The male and female. Make two for handbag panels, or put a large monogram on the second panel. Make a gusset 3½ inches wide. Canvas size 12–14

Four Birds
Cardinal, kingfisher, scarlet tanager, and wren. Canvas size 14

Pheasants
Detail from the Unicorn Tapestries.
Canvas size 14

Oriole
Canvas size 12–14

Seagulls
Canvas size 14–18

Peacock Feather
Canvas size 12–18

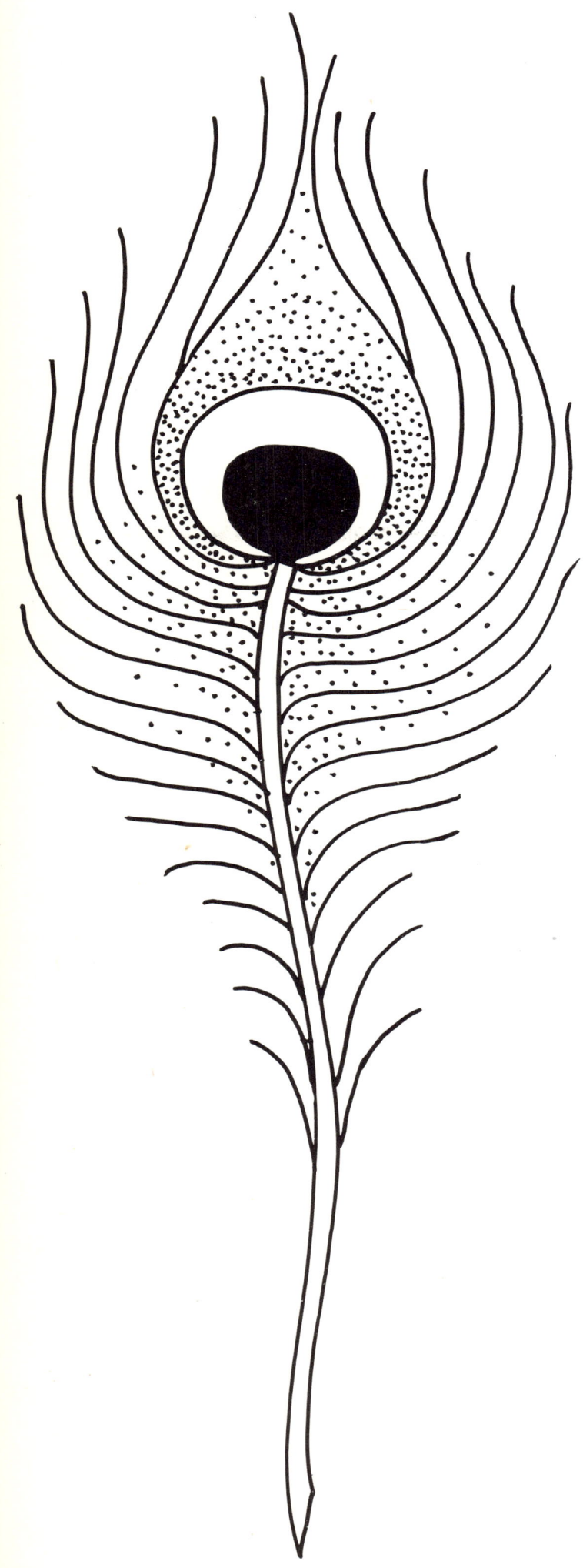

Partridges
Detail from the Unicorn Tapestries.
Canvas size 14

*Mother Owl and Chick
The owls' chests can be done in a simple bargello pattern to suggest feathers. The sky can be done in an ornamental stitch such as the Parisian, brick, leaf, or fern. Canvas size 10 if done all in tent stitch; 12–14 if done with an ornamental stitch*

*Owls
Canvas size 12–14*

Owl
Canvas size 12–14

Mythological Bird
Canvas size 12–14

Duck Decoy
Canvas size 10–14

Penguins
Canvas size 12–14

Hatching Chicks
Pincushion or coaster. Canvas size 18

Hen
Canvas size 14–18

Hen and Chicks
Eyeglass case if opening is on one end; small multipurpose case if opening is on the side. Repeat hen and chick by placing other half of canvas over design, or put a monogram or name on the other side. Canvas size 13

Animals

Rabbit
Canvas size 14

Cat
Stuffed toy or weighted doorstop.
Sample, page 201. Canvas size 10

Persian Cat
Canvas size 10–12

Tiger
Canvas size 14–18

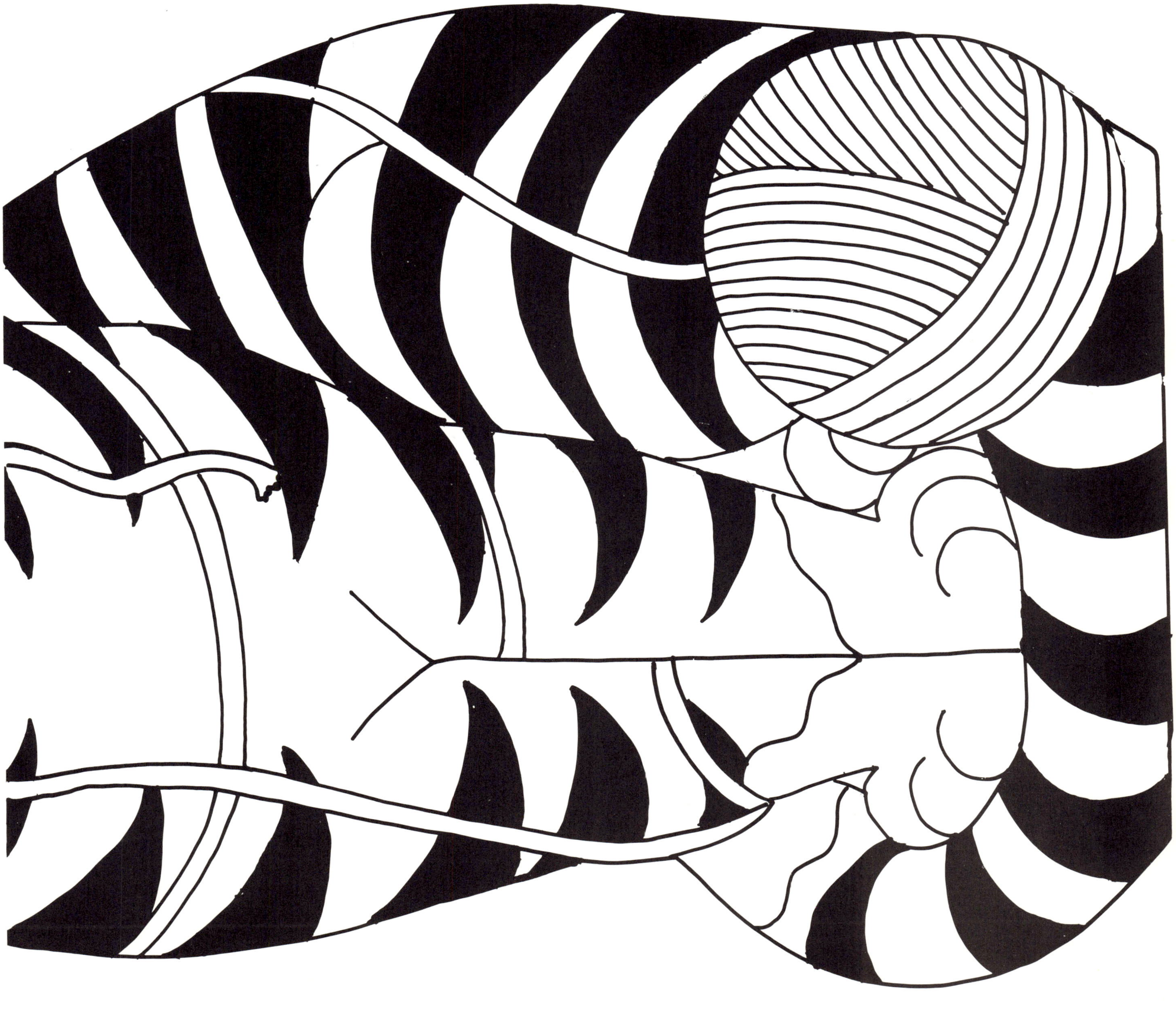

Sleeping Cat
Front of a tea cozy or semicircular pillow. Design for back, pages 74–75.
Canvas size 10

Sleeping Cat
Back of the tea cozy or pillow on pages 72–73.

Tabby Cat
Canvas size 14

Squirrels with Leaves and Nuts
Band for a box bag. Adjust length according to size of bag. Canvas size 14

Squirrel
Detail from the Unicorn Tapestries.
Shade the leaves with three or four
greens. Canvas size 14

Chipmunk
Canvas size 12–14

Koala Bears
Coaster or small pillow. Canvas size 14–18

Koala Bears
Mother and baby in a eucalyptus tree. Canvas size 14

Mouse with Flowers
Sachet or pincushion. Canvas size 18

Mouse in the Wheat
Canvas size 12–14

Mouse with Strawberry
A real novelty would be the body of the mouse done in shaded Turkey tufting and the strawberry in the double cross stitch with French knots for the seeds. Canvas size 12–14

Mice and Cheese
This design fits the Sudberry House tray. Canvas size 12–14

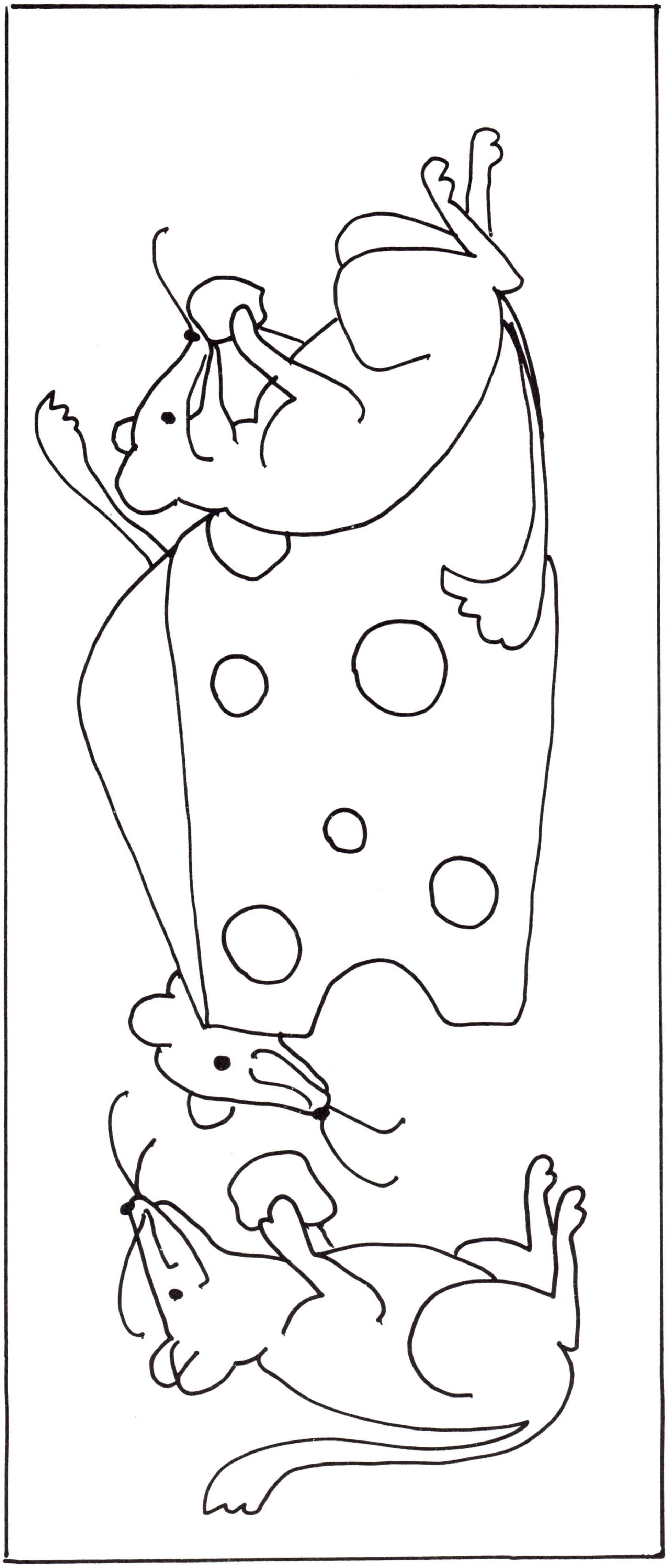

Frog on Lily Pad
Fits the Sudberry tray. Canvas size 12–14

Mother Bear and Cub
Canvas size 14

Kangaroo with Baby
Canvas size 12–14

Doe and Fawn
Looks best with a border. Canvas size 12–14

Horse Heads
Canvas size 12–14

Horse
Canvas size 14

Mare and Colt
Canvas size 18

Dogs
Canvas size 14

Doberman Pinscher

Pug

Terrier

French Poodle

87

Raccoon
Try a vertical stripe stitch for the background, for example, the fern, stem, or long-armed cross stitch. Canvas size 18

Elephants
Eyeglass case if open on the end; small multipurpose case if open on the side. Canvas size 14–18

Toad
This creature sits on a toadstool sniffing a flower. Sachet. Canvas size 18

Pig
Canvas size 12–14

Medieval Lady with Cat
Use a fancy stitch with a diagonal direction (Milanese, Byzantine, etc.) for the background. Canvas size 12–14

George Washington
From American folk art. Canvas size
12–14

*St. George and the Dragon
From a Russian icon. This design makes a nice wall hanging or banner. A combination of fancy stitches is very effective. For example, use mosaic or Parisian stitch for the land; Gobelin over two for the horse; Byzantine, Milanese, Hungarian ground, or jacquard for the sky. Fill in St. George's jacket with long upright stitches to look like quilting. Make at least two borders of different sizes and colors using, for example, the cashmere stitch and the long-armed cross stitch. Sample, page 204.
Canvas size 12–14*

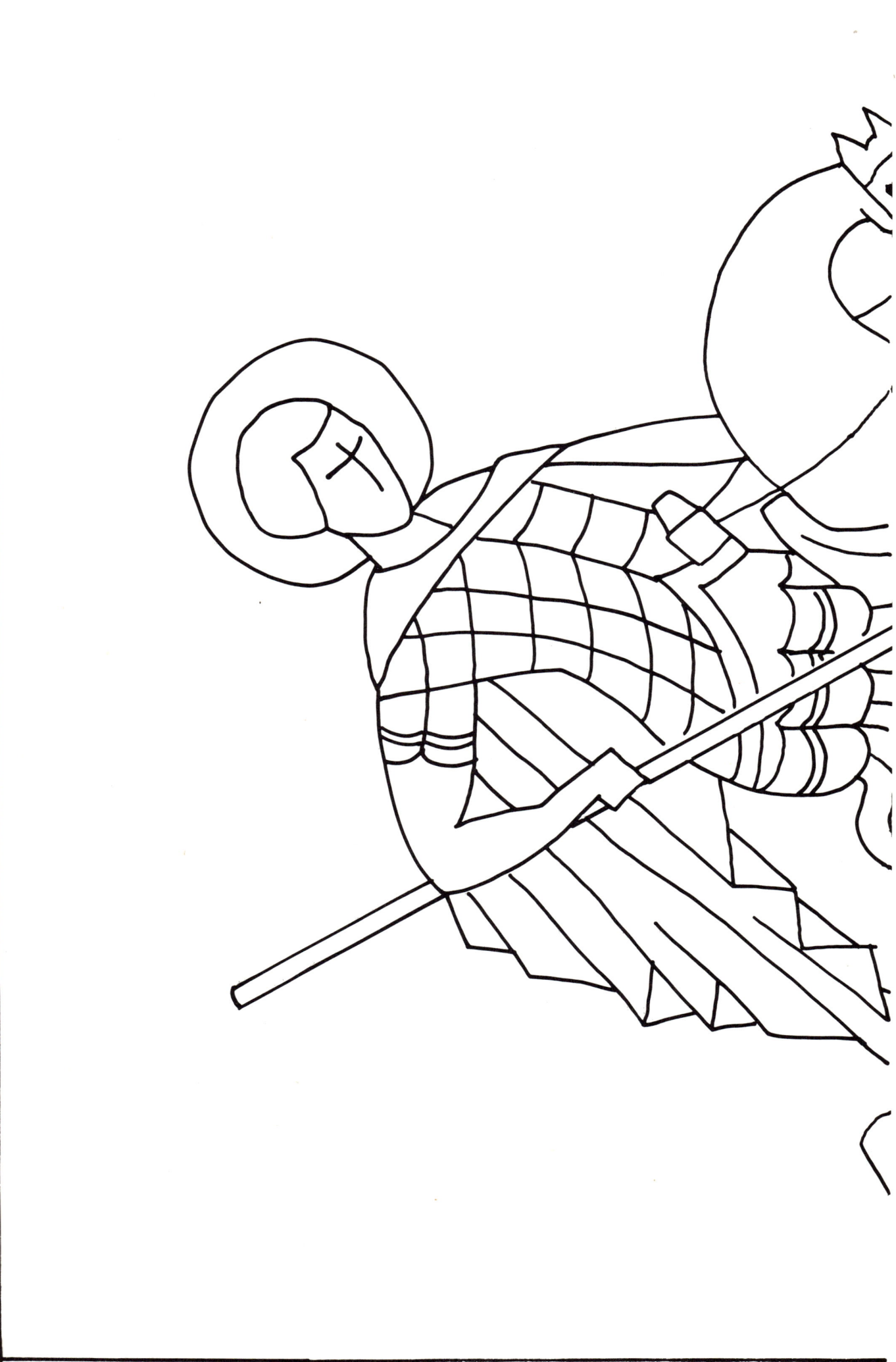

Hunting Hound
Detail from the Unicorn Tapestries.
Canvas size 14

Two Rabbits
Details from the Unicorn Tapestries.
Canvas size 12–14

Persian Deer
Round pillow. Canvas size 12–14

Monkeys
Canvas size 12–14

Insects

Spider and Web
Canvas size 12–14

Butterfly
Surround with a fancy stitch or plain border and fold in center to make a checkbook cover. Sample on the cover.
Canvas size 14

Butterflies and Flowers
Canvas size 14

Bugs
Motifs for belts, coasters, luggage straps, ties, little cases. Canvas size 14–18

Butterflies
These would look nice with a border.
Canvas size 14–18

Sea Creatures

Sea Creatures
Canvas size 10–18

Sea Creatures
Handbag. Make a gusset 2½ inches wide. Sample, page 199 and on the cover. Canvas size 14

Dolphins
These would look nice with a border. The Greek key border in the sample has to be counted out. Sample, page 205. Canvas size 12

Shells
Eyeglass case. Canvas size 18

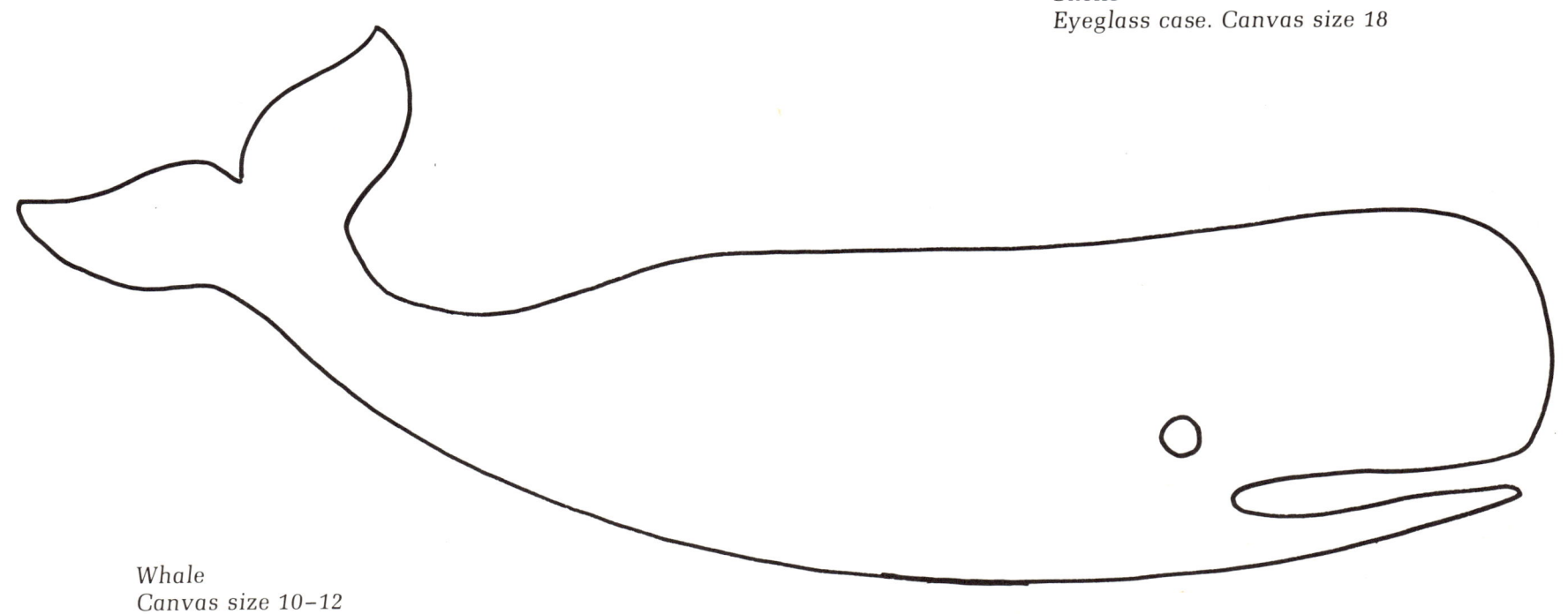

Whale
Canvas size 10–12

Fruits, Vegetables, and Kitchen Motifs

Fruits and Vegetables
Motifs for belts, coasters, luggage straps, pincushions, eyeglass cases, etc. Canvas size 12–18

Onions, Green Pepper, Garlic
Canvas size 12–18

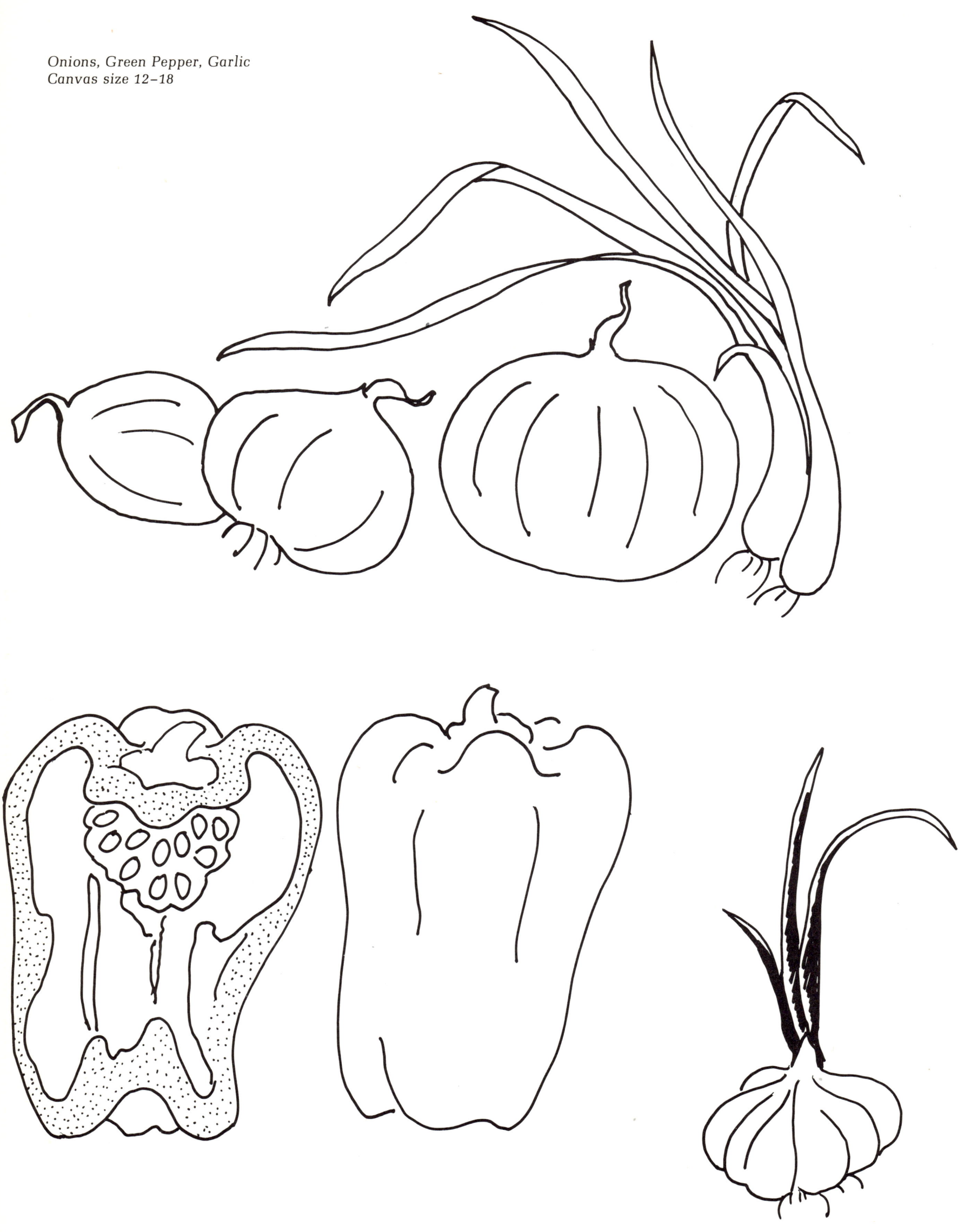

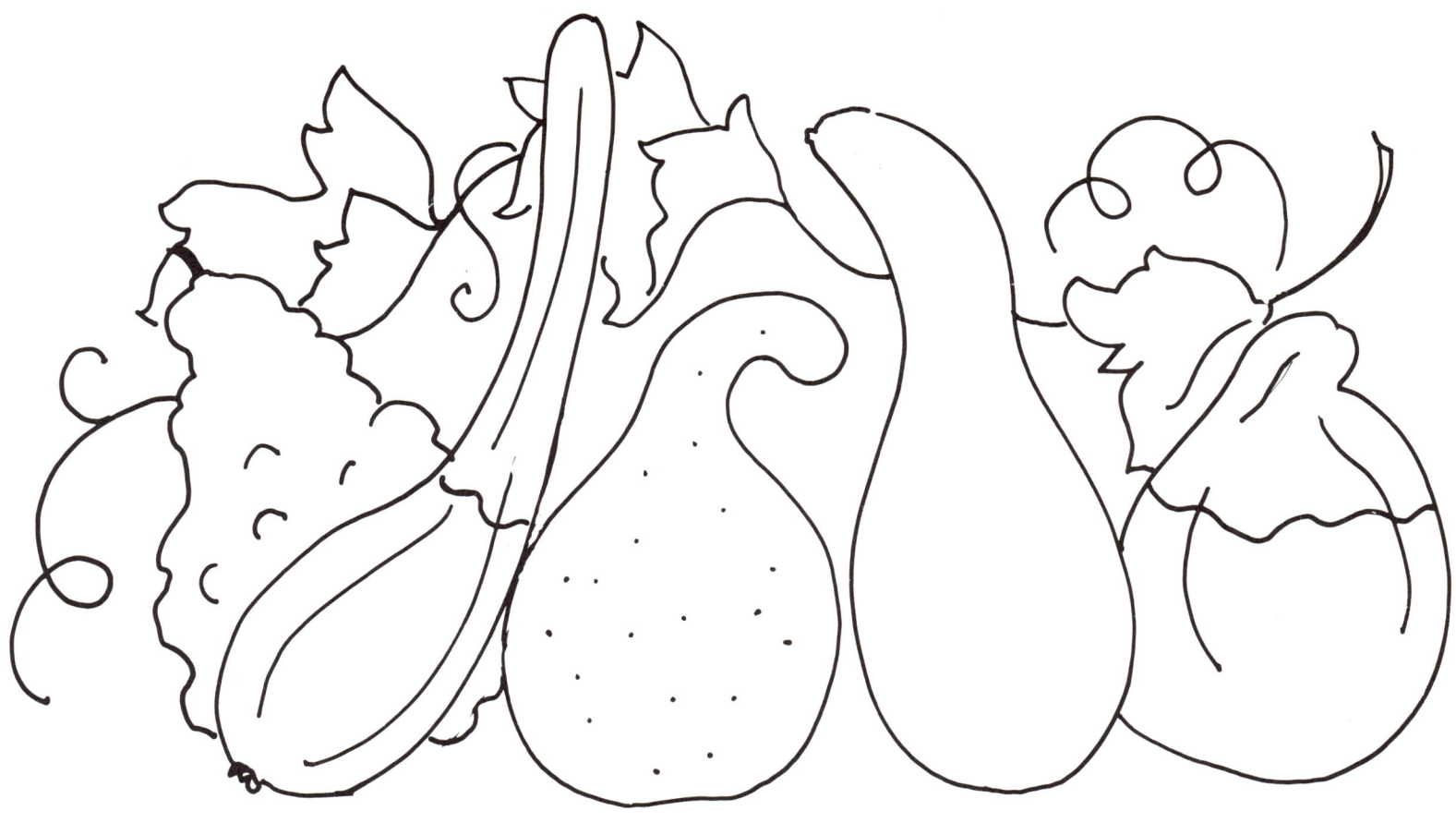

Gourds
Canvas size 14

Pumpkins and Fruits
Nice with a border. Canvas size 12–14

Fruits and Vegetables
Canvas size 12–18

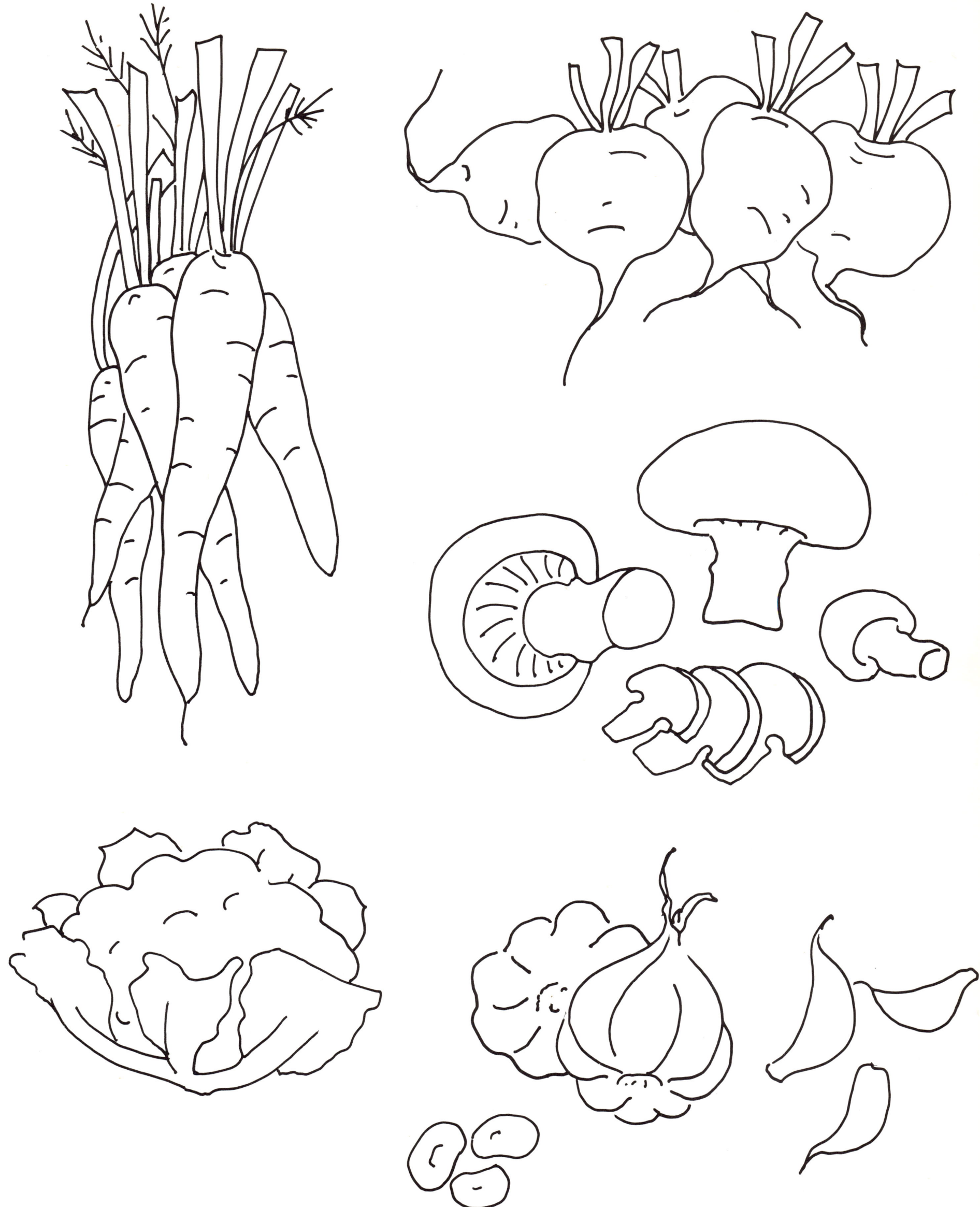

Breakfast
This would make a nice trivet or set of placemats. Canvas size 12–14

Kitchen Motifs
Canvas size 14–18

Thanksgiving Turkey
Canvas size 18

Birthday Cake
Canvas size 18

Toaster Cover
Make sure designs are on background large enough to fit sides of toaster. Join with fabric gusset and cording. Canvas size 12–14

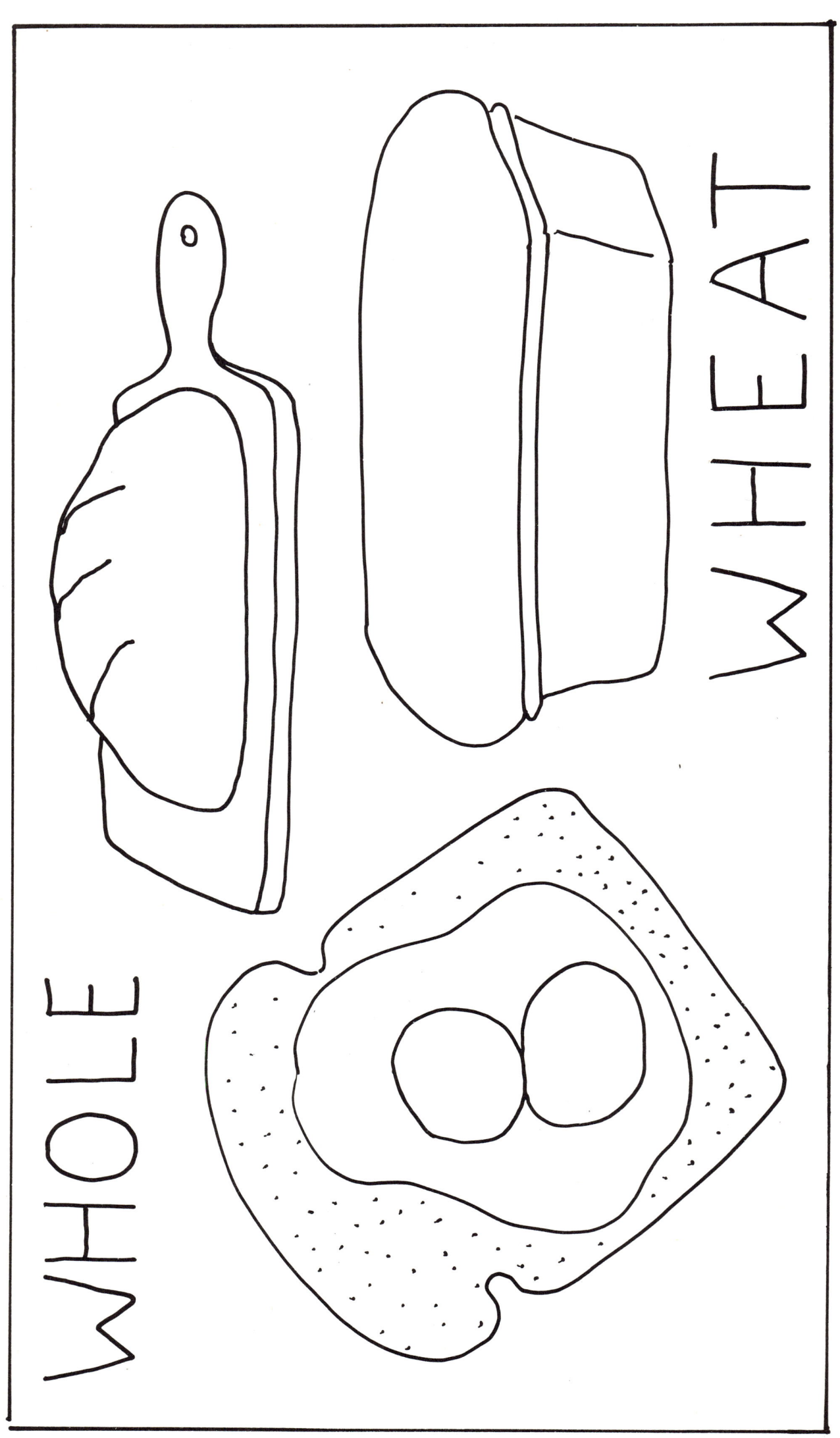

Transportation

Antique Bicycle
Canvas size 12

Packard, 1911
Canvas size 14

Classic Cars
Canvas size 14–18

Dump Truck
Canvas size 12–14

Classic Car
Canvas size 14–18

School Bus
Canvas size 12–14

Volkswagen
Canvas size 12–14

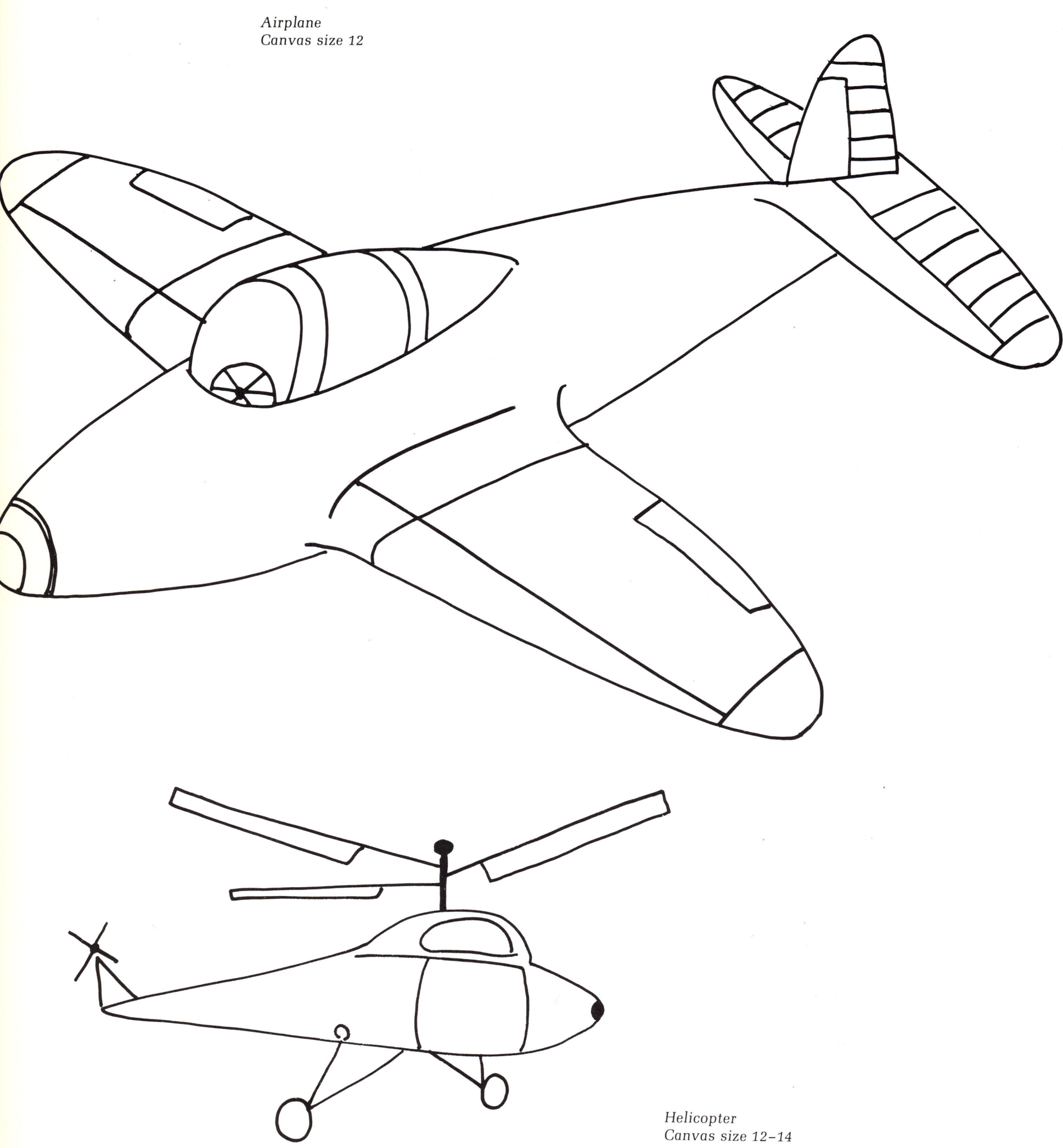

Airplane
Canvas size 12

Helicopter
Canvas size 12–14

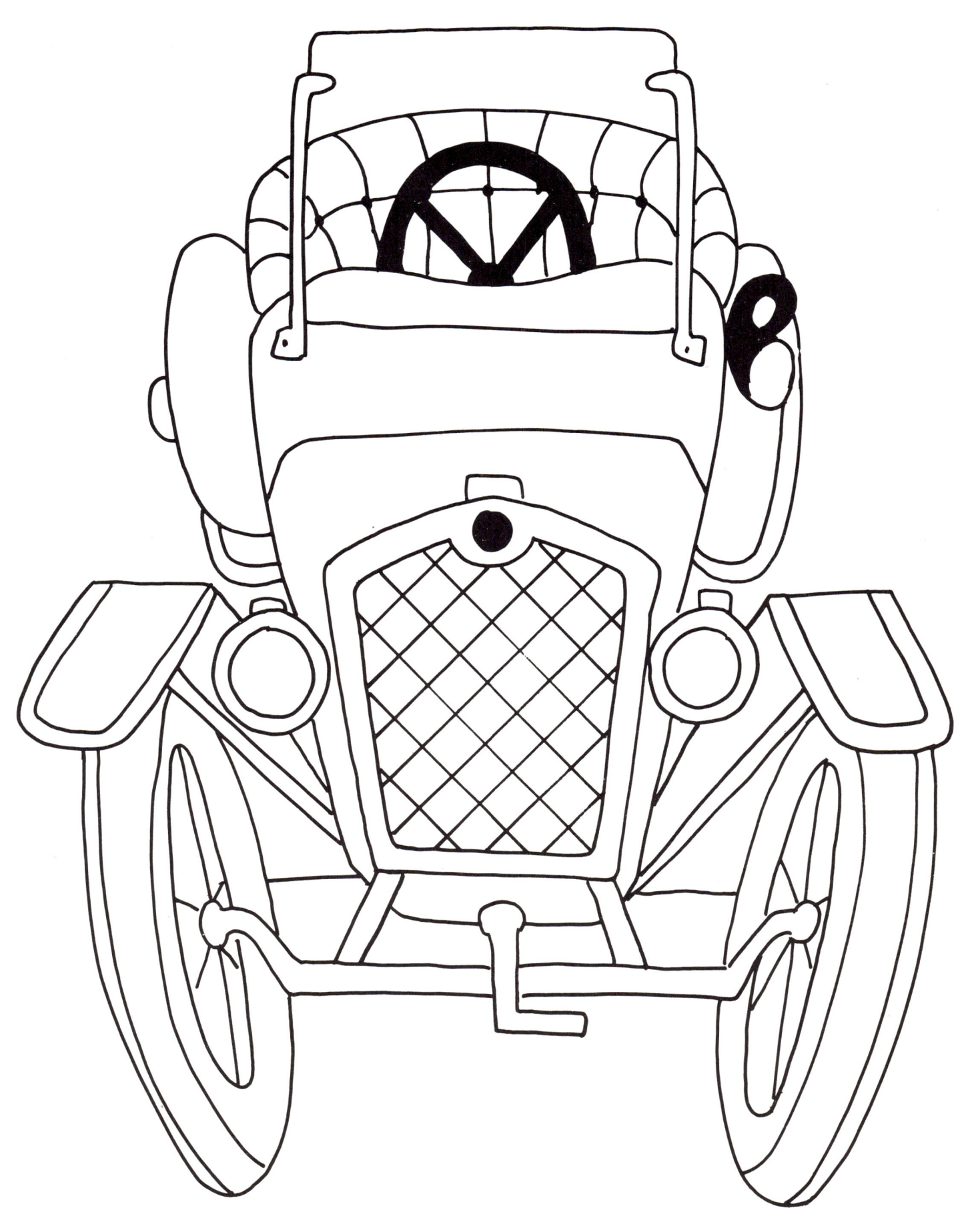

Roadster
Try an ornamental stitch such as
Scotch or mosaic stitch for the grille.
Canvas size 14

Circus Wagon
Use bright colors. Canvas size 14

Lady and Hackney
Canvas size 12–14

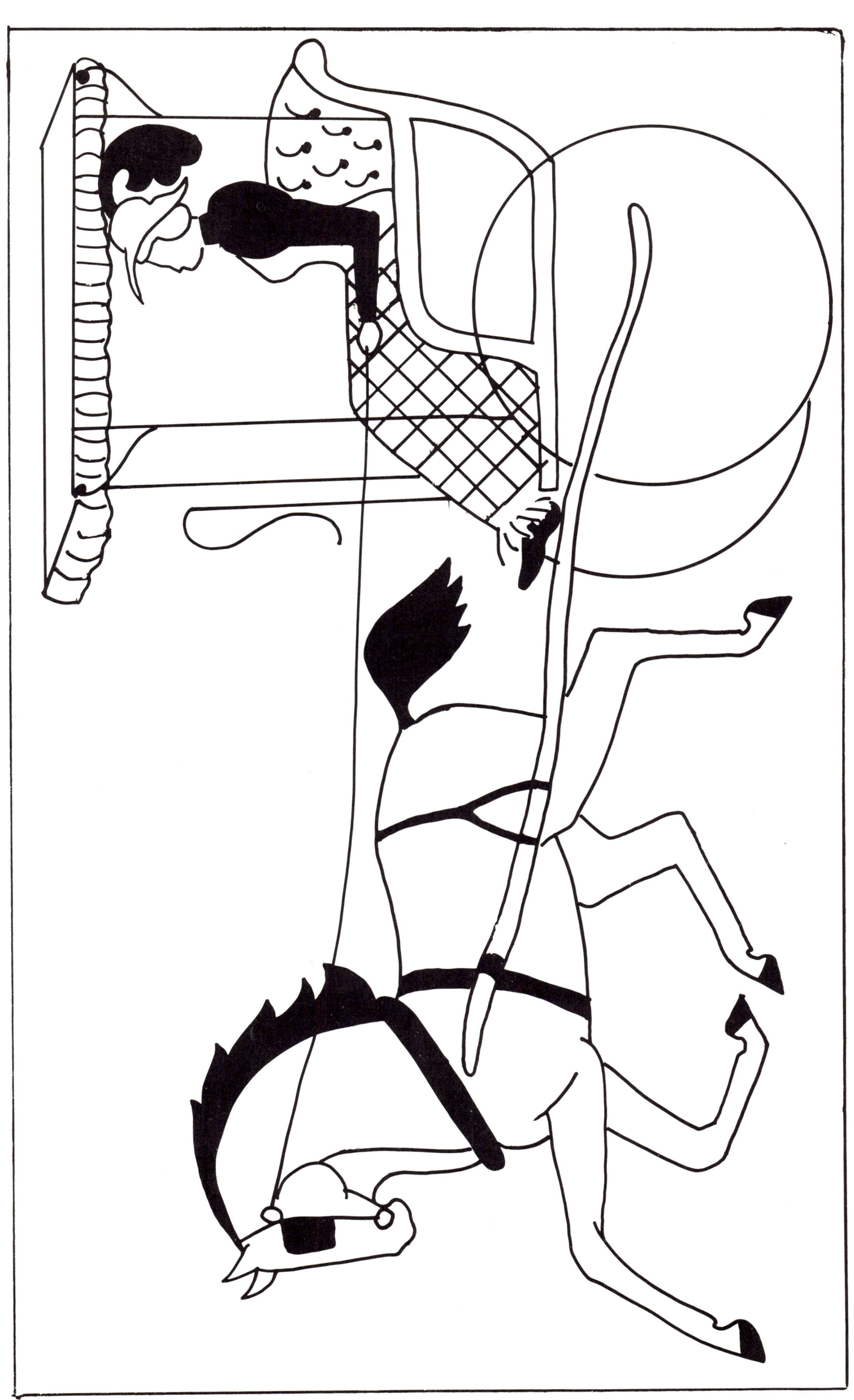

125

Victorian Baby Stroller
Canvas size 12–14

Galleon
Canvas size 14

Sailing Ship
Canvas size 12–14

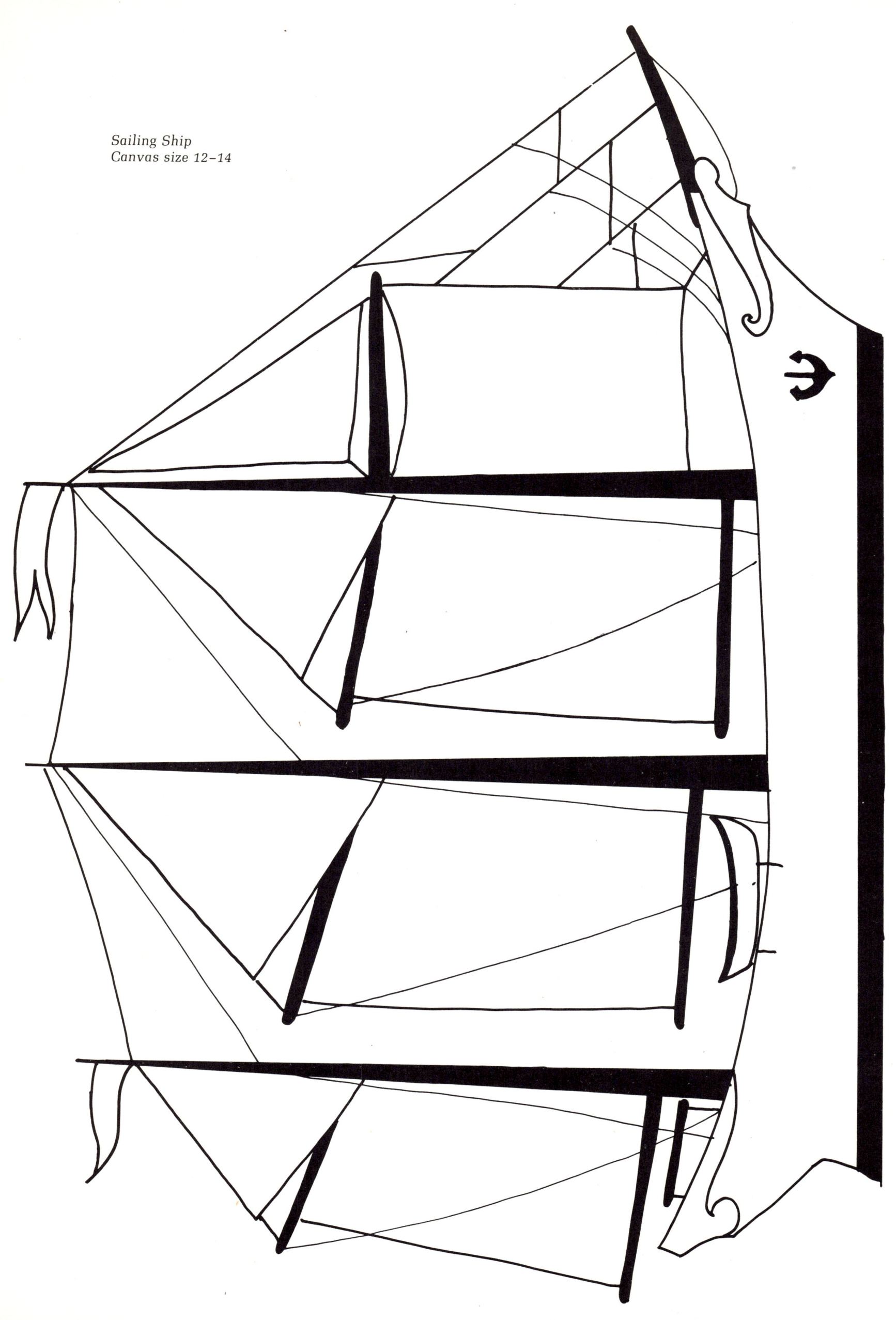

Locomotive
The rivets would be nice in French knots. Canvas size 12

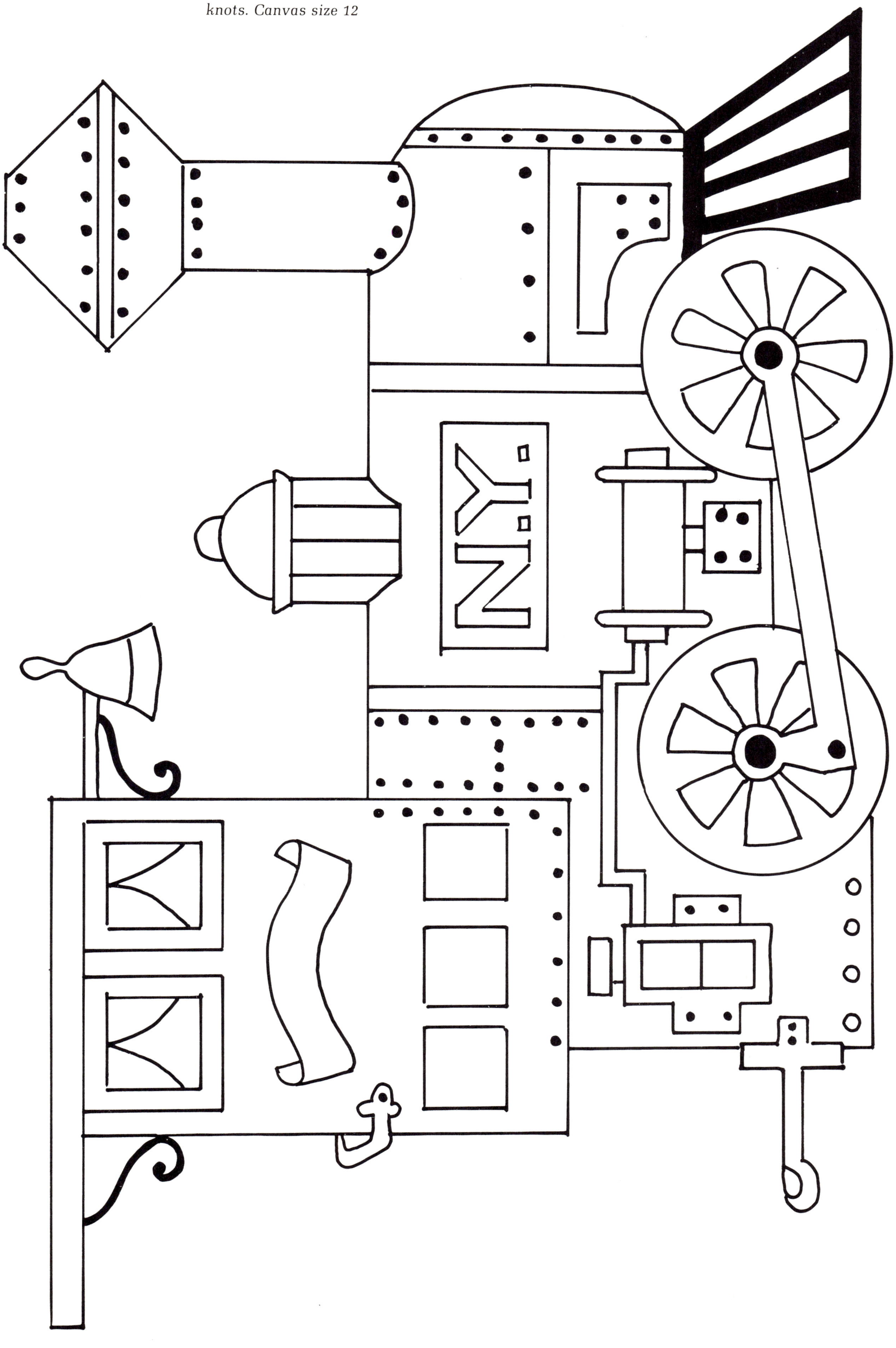

Fire Engine
Use fancy stitch border. Canvas size 12

Religious Subjects and Holidays

Matzoh Cover
The motif is grapes and vines. A project for the skilled embroiderer who wants a very formal piece of work, this design can be done with gold or silver threads on velvet. In needlepoint silk threads for the design, with a wool background, would be very beautiful. An ornamental stitch could be used for the background and borders. In needlepoint the design area should be at least 16 inches square. The design looks best with a border.
Canvas size 14–18

Noah's Ark
See page 138 for complete design.

Noah's Ark
See page 138 for complete design.

Noah's Ark
Makes a rug, wall hanging, picture, stool cover, large pillow, or the front panel for a large wedge-shaped reading pillow. Use plain or fancy border. Some stitch suggestions: Byzantine or Jacquard stitch for the roof of the ark; Gobelin alternating in rows over two and over four threads for the boat; French knots for the lamb; Parisian stitch for the sky; and brick stitch, worked vertically, for the water.
Canvas size 12

Church Kneeler
*The lamb, symbol of Christ, surrounded by the emblems of the four evangelists. The side panels make a self-gusset and fold down to form a cushion that is an individual church kneeler. On the outside edges leave three inches of canvas beyond stitching area to provide for a turn under. Since the gusset has a busy pattern, it might be interesting to do the background of the cushion in an ornamental stitch such as the Hungarian ground or cashmere stitch.
Canvas size 12–14*

Church Kneeler
See page 139 for complete design.

Church Kneeler
See page 139 for complete design.

Christmas Ornaments
Little things to hang on the tree or appliqué. Sample, page 200 and on the cover. Most will work well on number 14 canvas but the more detailed ones require number 18.

Christmas Stocking
Put child's name or initials in the space at the top of the stocking. Canvas size 14

Christmas Ornaments
More things to hang on the tree or appliqué. Sample, page 200 and on the cover. Most will work well on number 14 canvas but the more detailed ones require number 18.

Pennsylvania Dutch Heart
Makes a delightful candy box cover or a cushion with a gusset like a box pillow. Canvas size 10–14

Heraldry

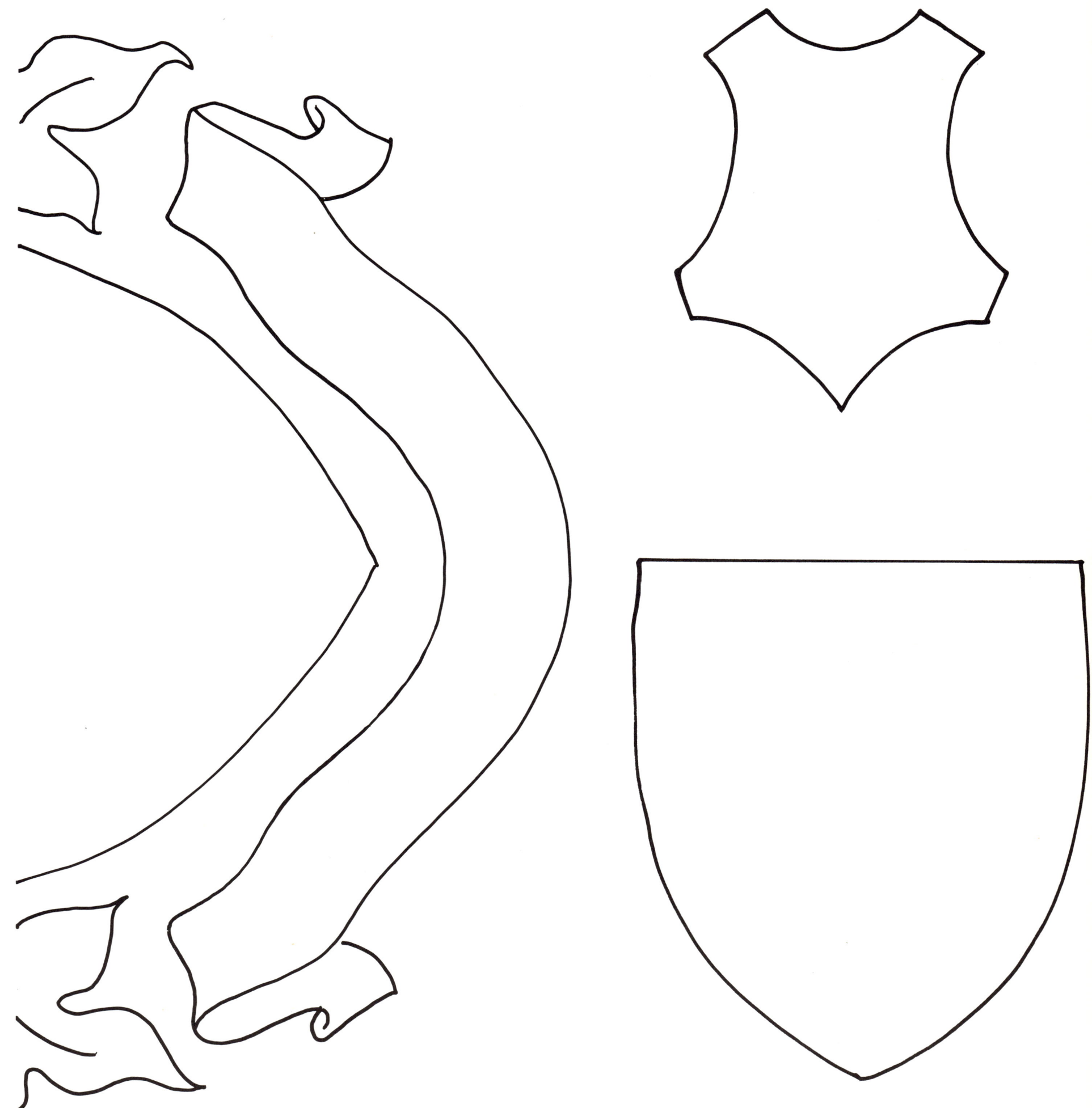

Coat-of-arms Shield
Fill with your own device and motto.
Canvas size 14–18

Heraldic Griffin
Canvas size 14

Heraldic Motifs
Small designs to make up your own coat-of-arms. Canvas size 14–18

Medieval Castle
Try mosaic stitch for the land; Hungarian ground for the sky; Scotch stitch for the background with the keys. Sample, page 205 and on the cover. Canvas size 18

Heraldic Unicorn
Canvas size 14

Heraldic Lion
Canvas size 14

Heraldic Lion and Unicorn
Canvas size 10–14

American Eagle
A banner, wall hanging, stool or bench cover. Try a border of stars using the stars in the design. Canvas size 12–14

Sports and Hobbies

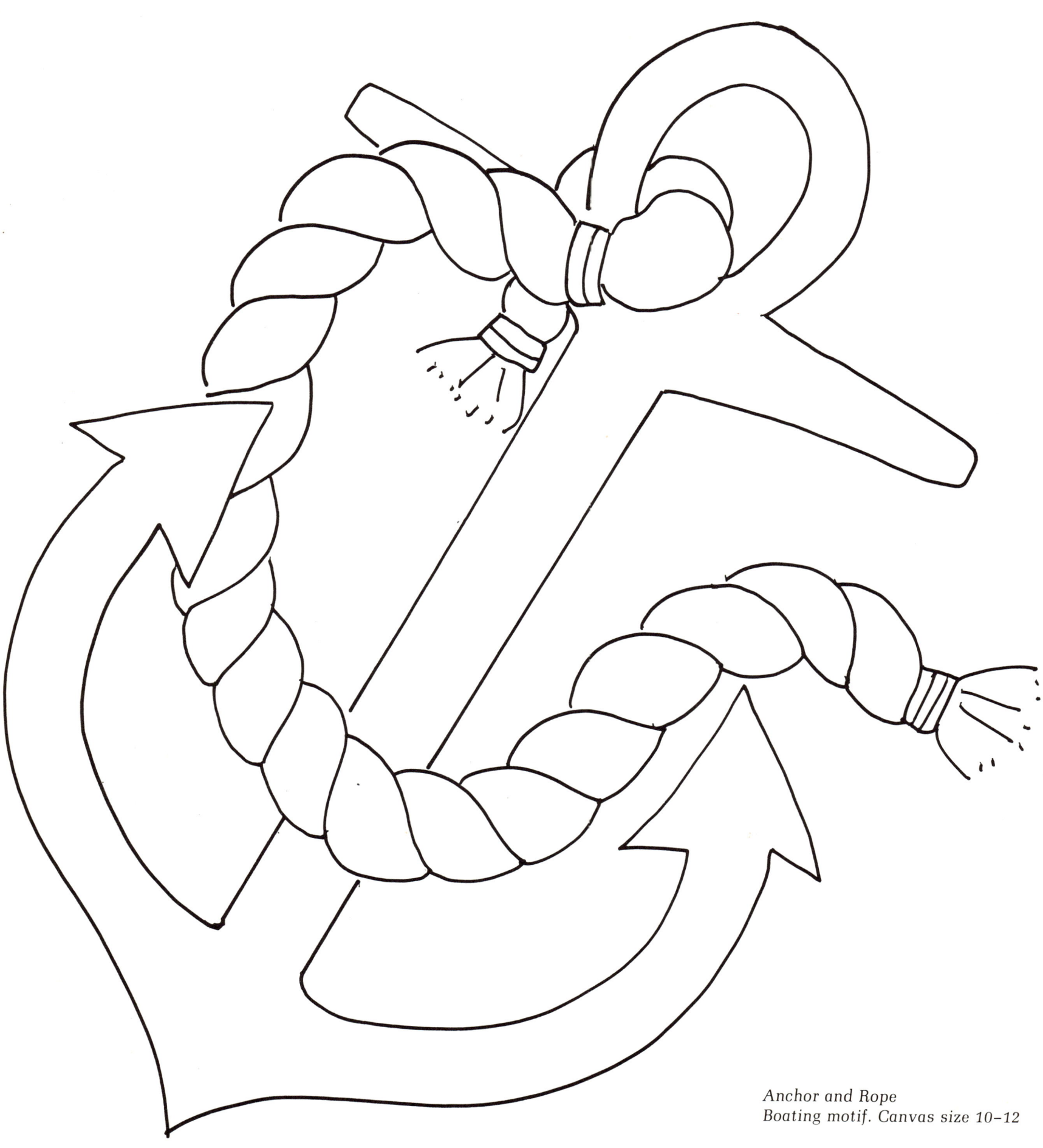

Anchor and Rope
Boating motif. Canvas size 10–12

Equestrian Motif
Canvas size 18

Fox Hunting
Horn and Mask. Canvas size 14–18

Tennis Racquet Cover
This design can be traced onto an already assembled zip-out canvas from a kit or can be sent to a professional finisher. Canvas size 12–14

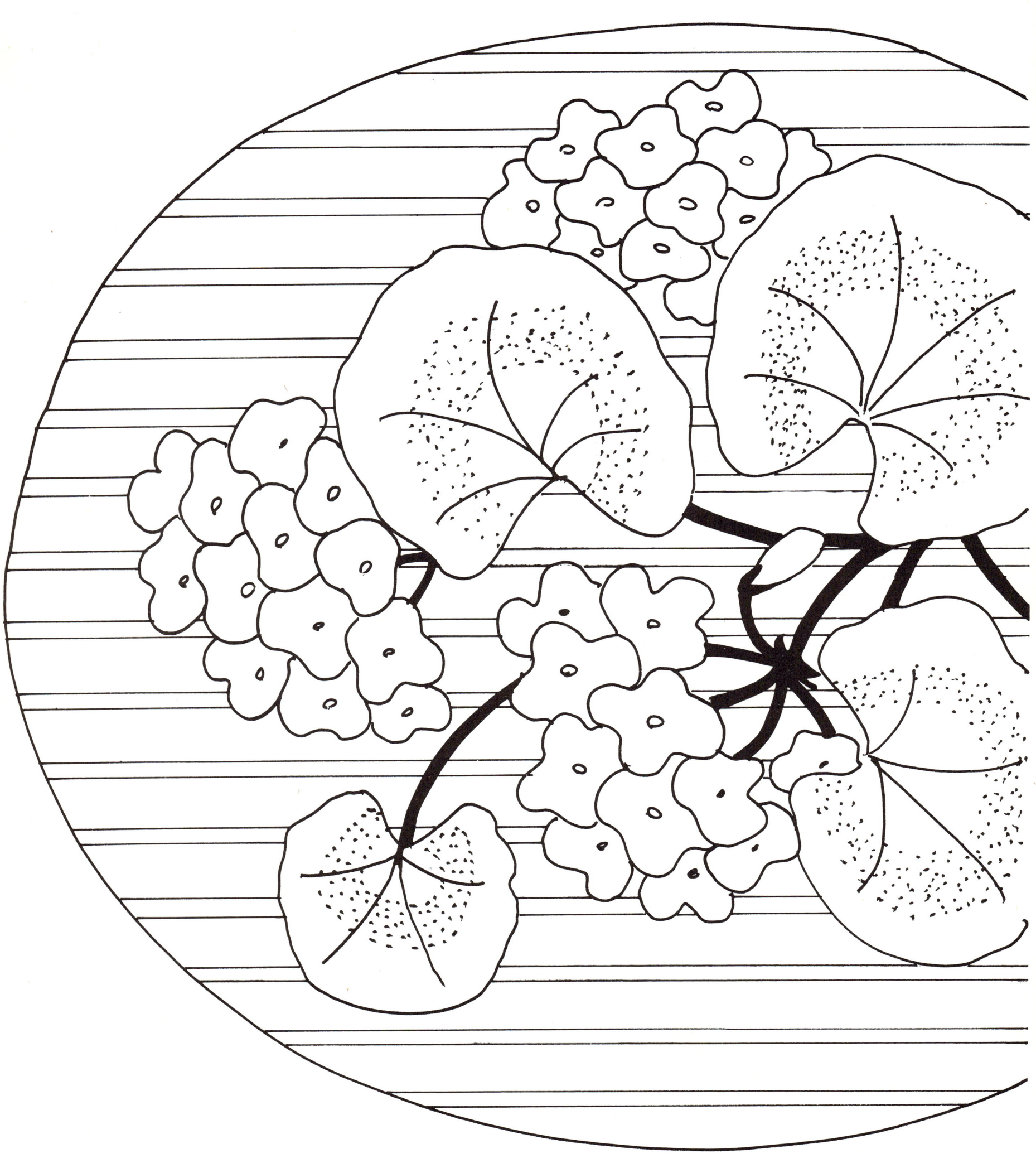

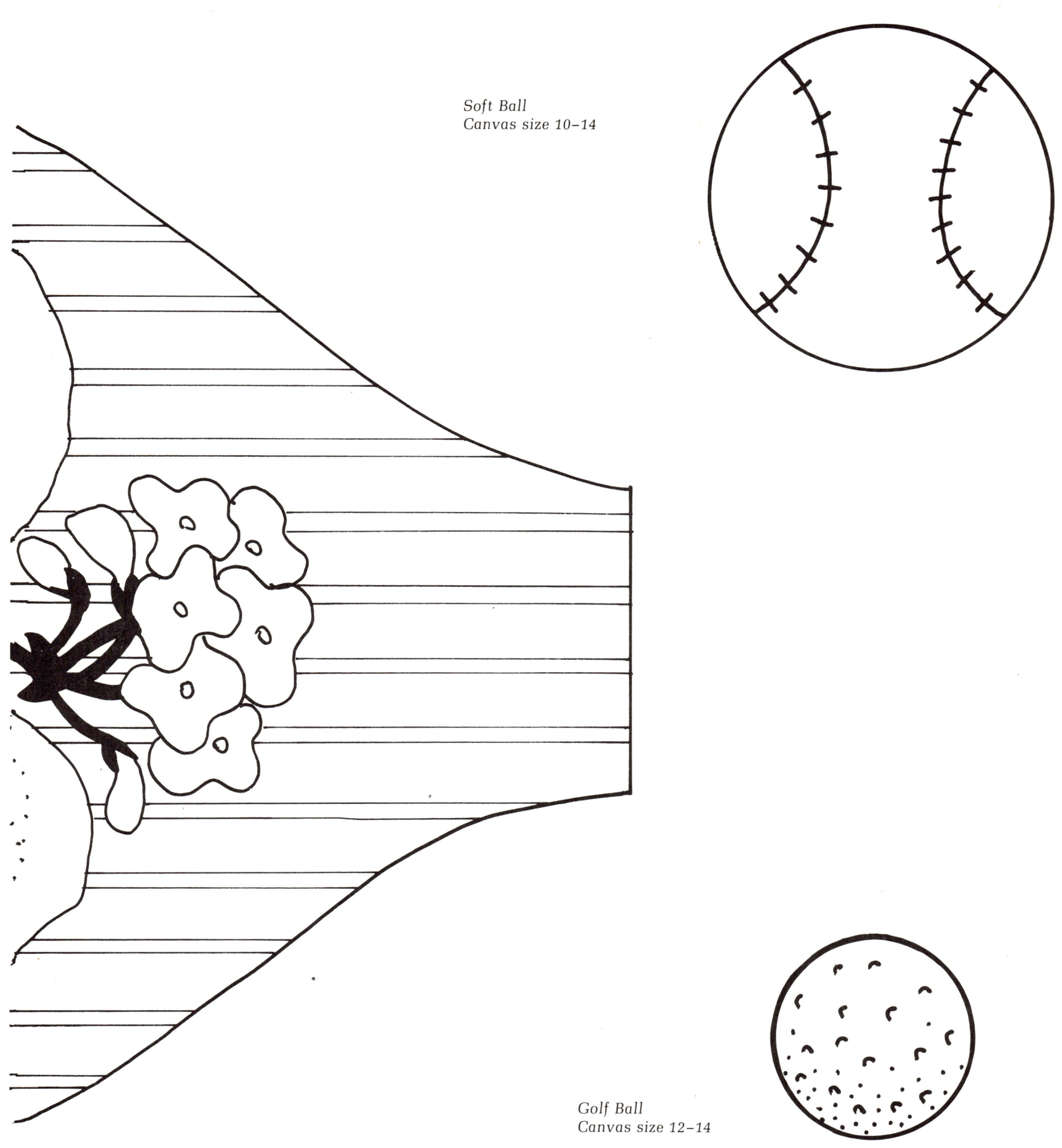

Soft Ball
Canvas size 10-14

Golf Ball
Canvas size 12-14

Musical Notes and Signs
Canvas size 10–18

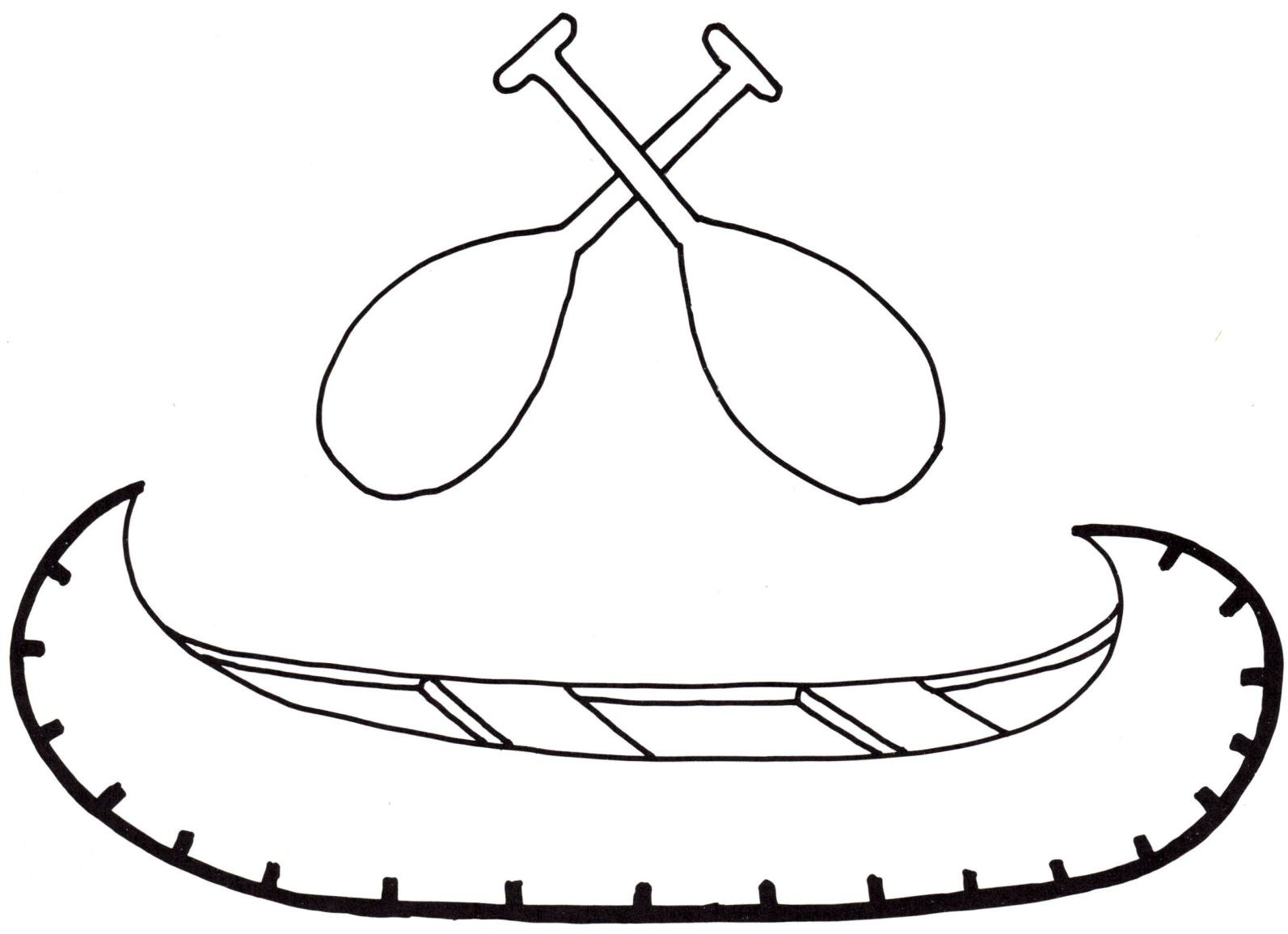

Canoe and Paddles
Canvas size 10–14

Playing Card Suits
Canvas size 10–14

Jack of Spades
A carrying case for playing cards or a tobacco pouch. Make other side in fabric or in needlepoint of same design or ornate monogram. For tobacco pouch, line with plastic, close with zipper. For playing card case, close with zipper or Velcro. Canvas size 14–18

Squash Racquet Case
Queen of Diamonds. Canvas size 14

Sporting Motifs
For belt, purse, pincushion, coasters,
etc. Canvas size 18

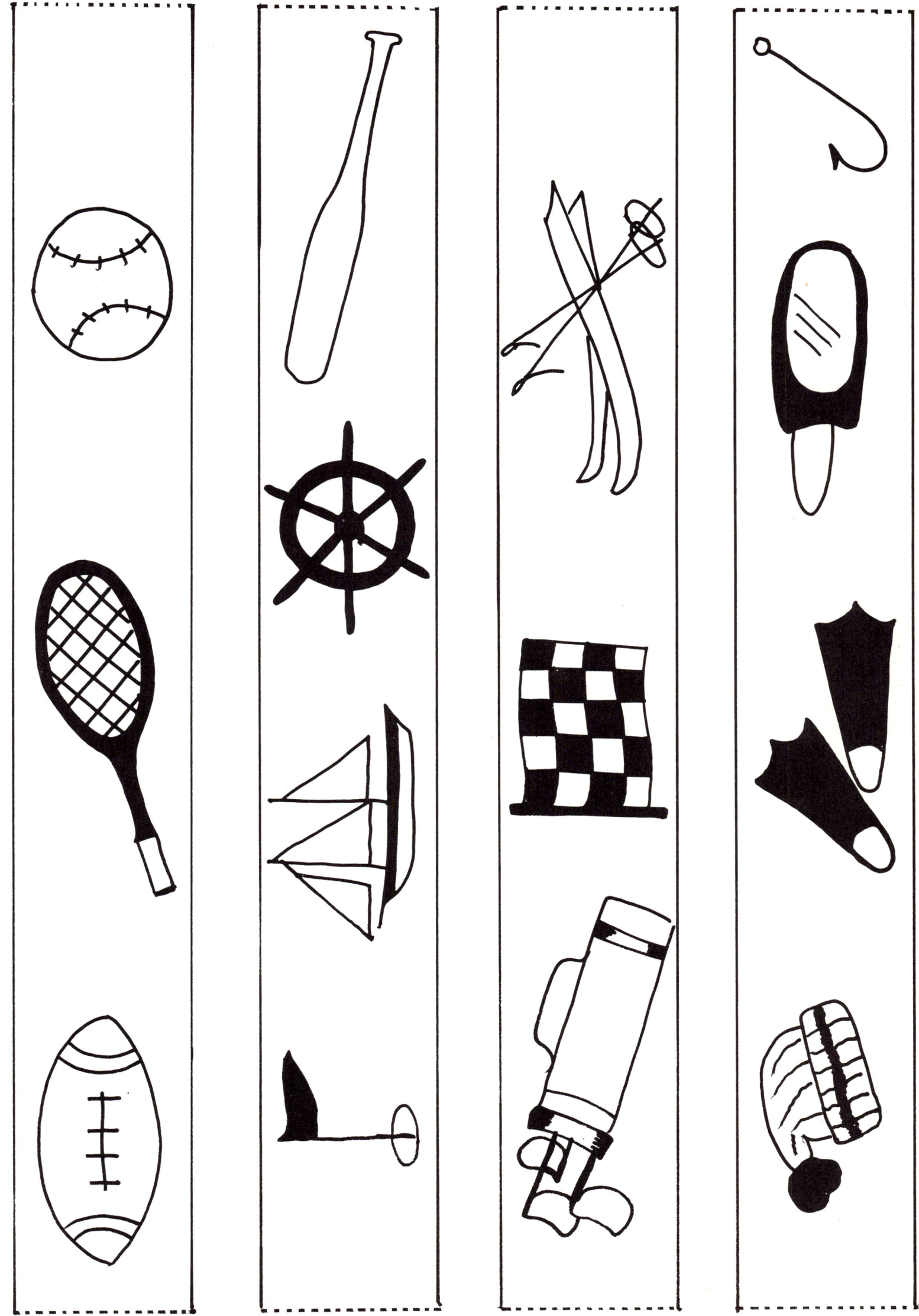

Country Life

Country Store
Canvas size 12–14

Farm Scene
Canvas size 14–18

Old Iron Stove
Canvas size 14

Oil Lamps
Canvas size 12–14

Miscellaneous Projects

Doll in Denim Jumper
Embroider orange top-stitching in wool or cotton over blue needlepoint. Features can be done in needlepoint if you use canvas size 14; embroider features over needlepoint if you use number 10 or 12 canvas. Do hair area in needlepoint. When doll is completed, make additional hair of long strands of wool attached to doll at dotted lines as shown in the diagram and tie into braids down the sides. Stuff doll. Canvas size 10–14

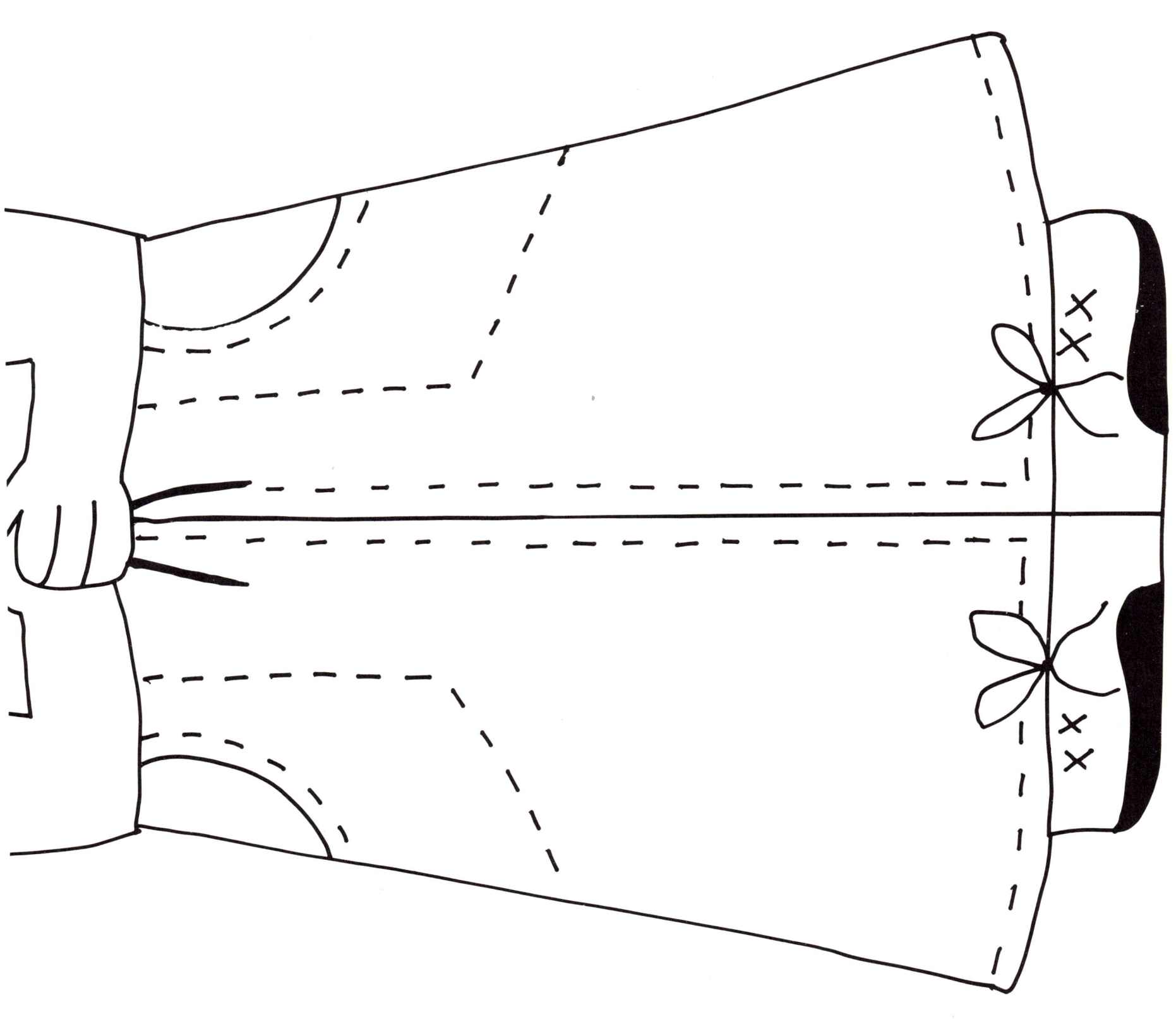

Block Toy
Child's animal and letter block. Fold on the dotted lines and sew to make a block. Canvas size 18

Scissors Cases
Two cases for embroidery scissors.
Canvas size 14–18

Eyeglass Case
Pennsylvania Dutch floral motif. Fold in center, leave open on end. Sample, page 201. Canvas size 14

Frame
Floral motif on a frame for mirror or picture. Canvas size 12

Clutch Bag
Diagonal geometric design: make all stripes conform to the true diagonal or bias weave of the canvas as occurs naturally with the diagonal tent or basketweave stitch. Put a monogram in the center. Sample, page 203 and on the cover. Canvas size 14

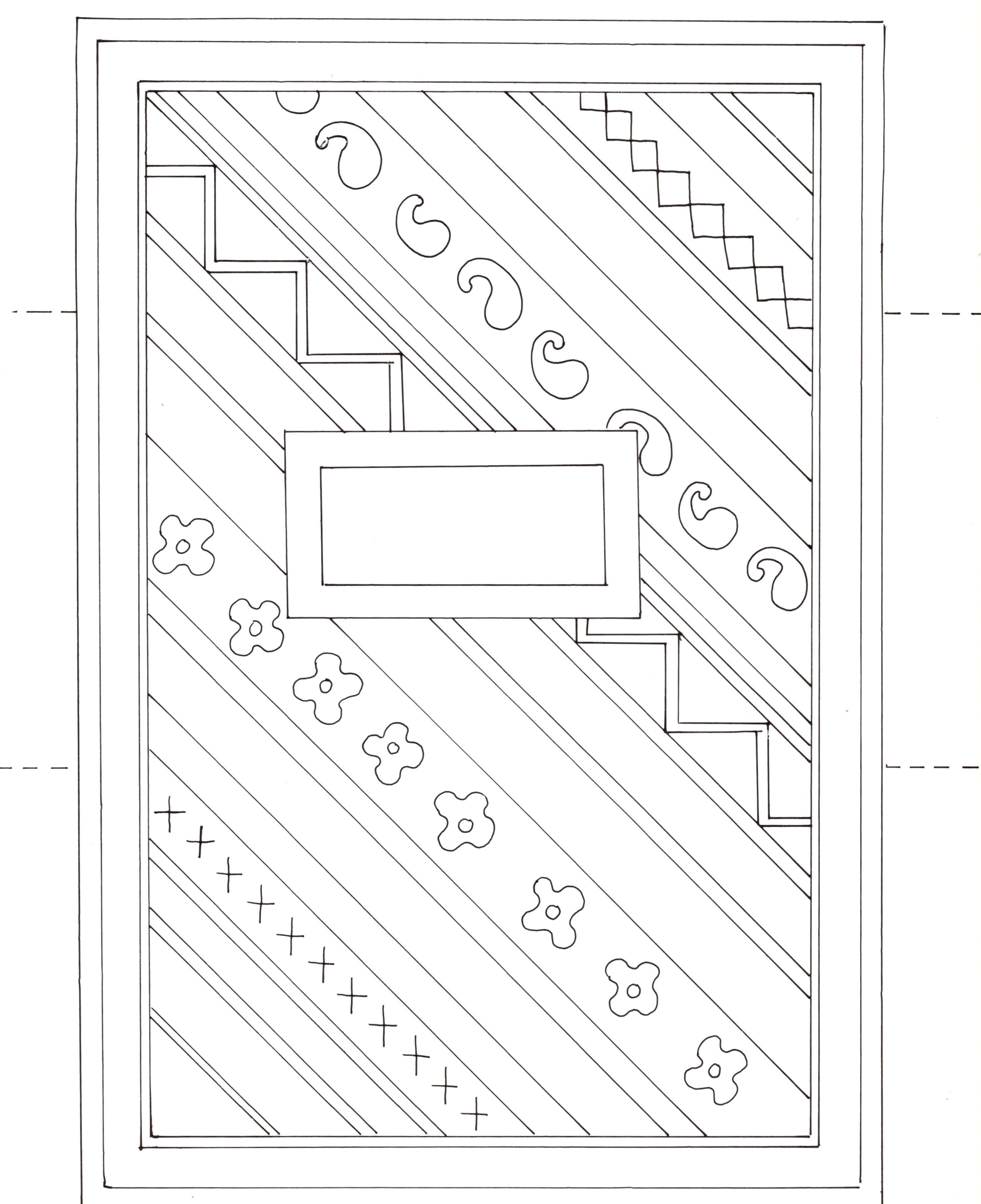

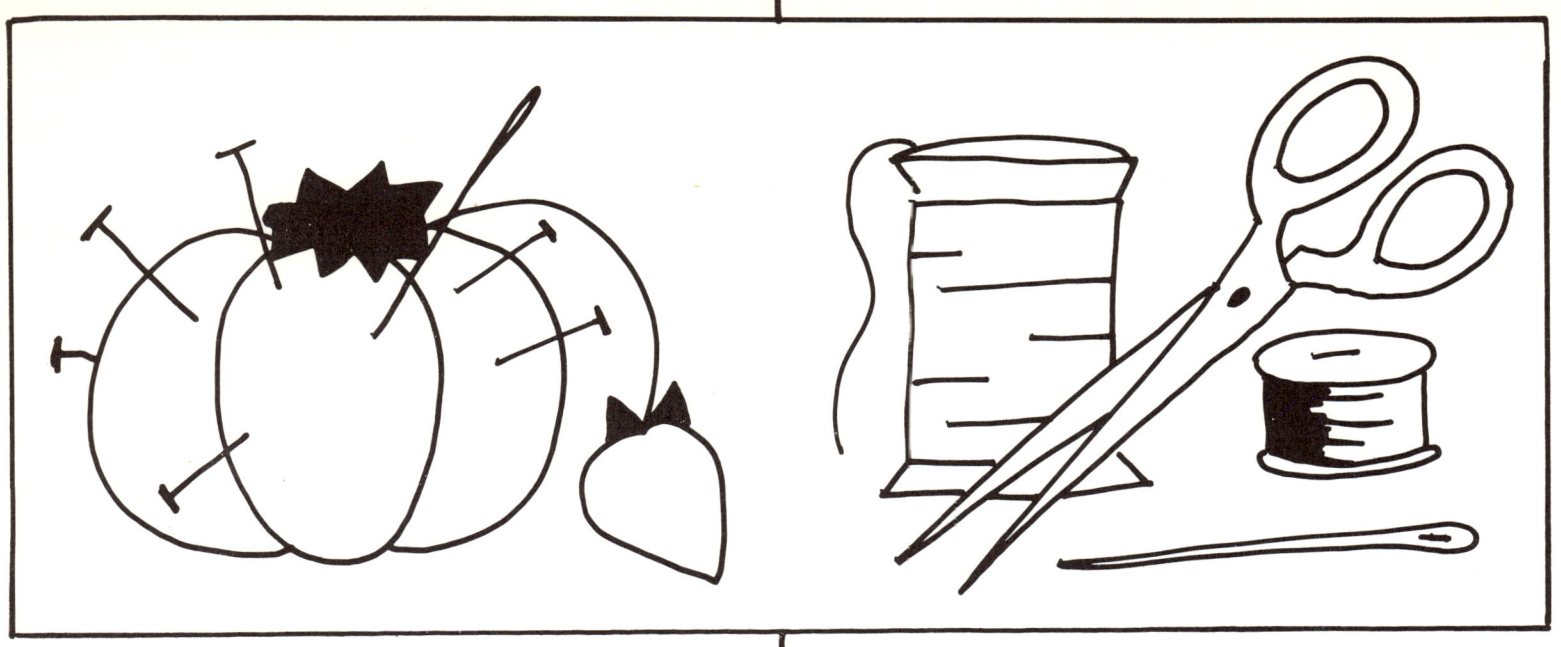

Needle Book
Fold in center, and sew in pinked flannel pages to hold needles. Canvas size 14

Dog Collar
Repeat motif to correct length. Back with felt and finish with purchased buckle. Canvas size 14–18

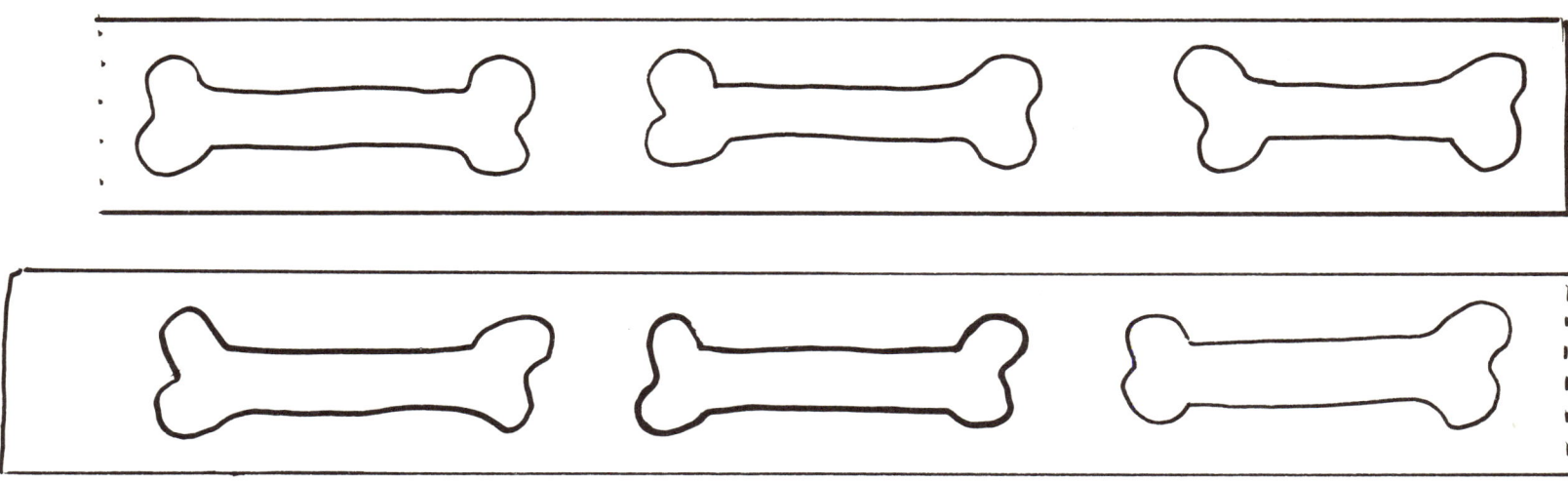

Needle Case
For knitting needles and crochet hooks. Fold down the center and close with a snap. Canvas size 12–14

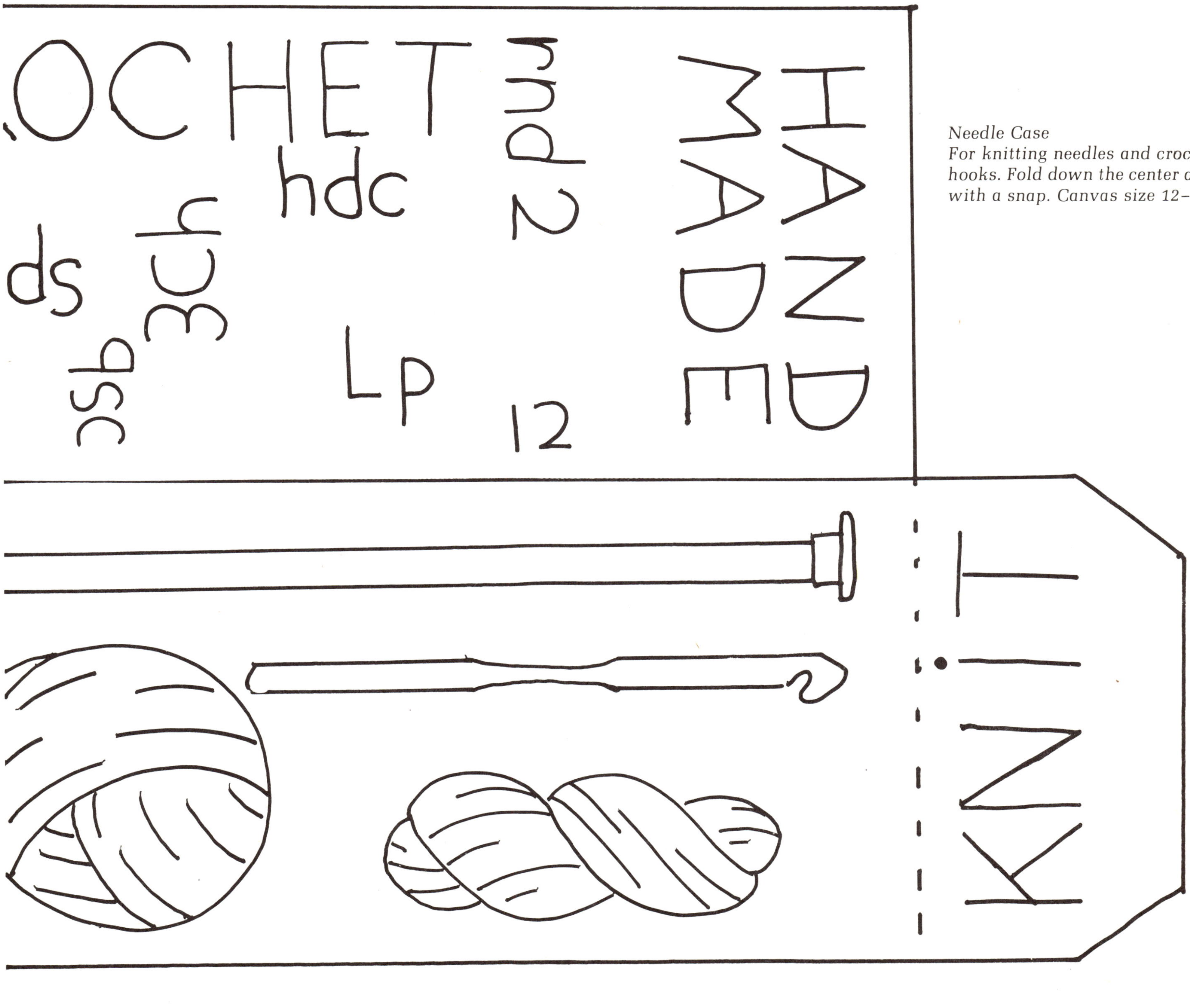

Cat Collar
Canvas size 18

Alphabets

Fancy Alphabet
Shown for canvas size 12 and 14, but can be reduced or enlarged as desired.

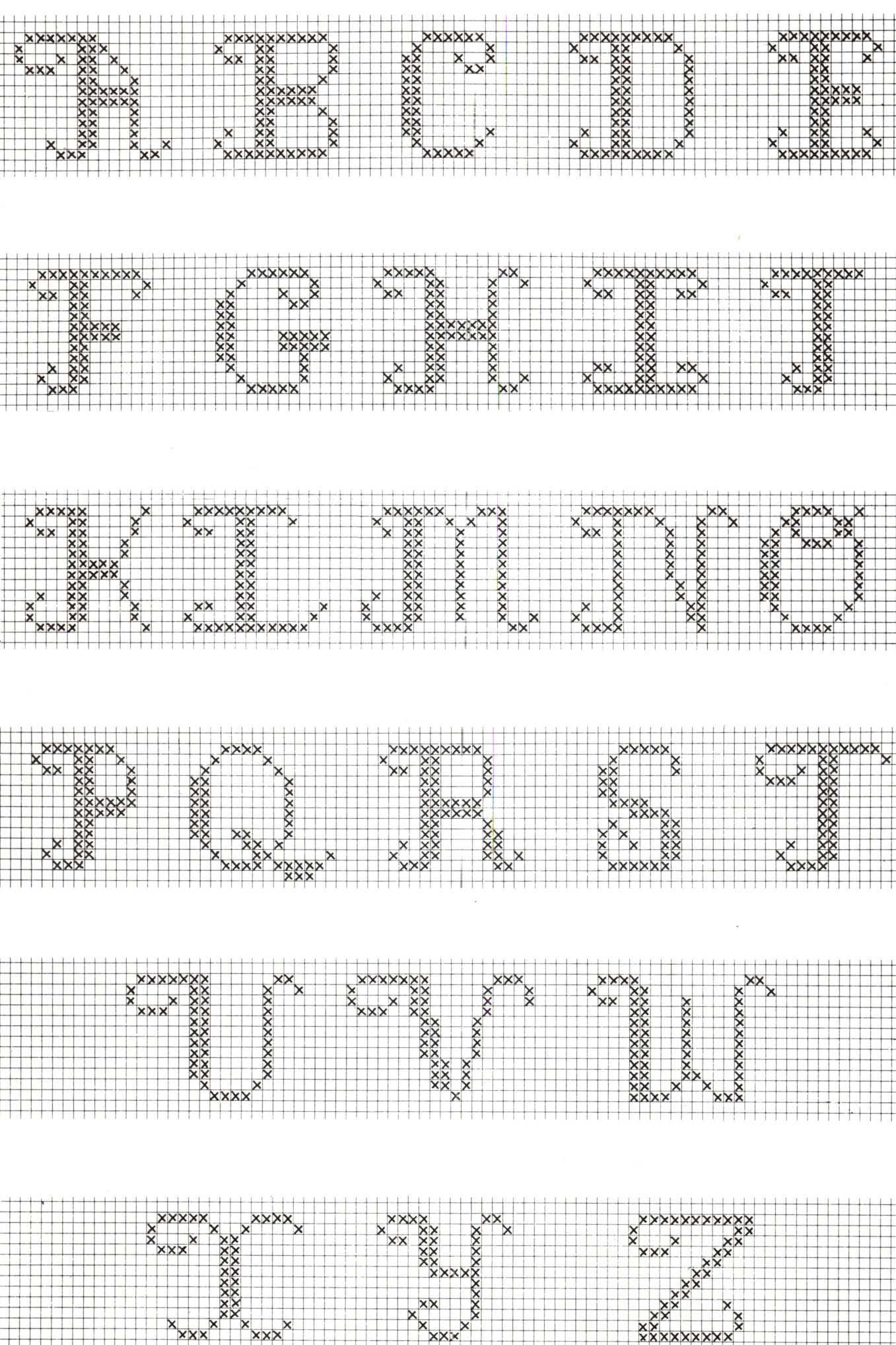

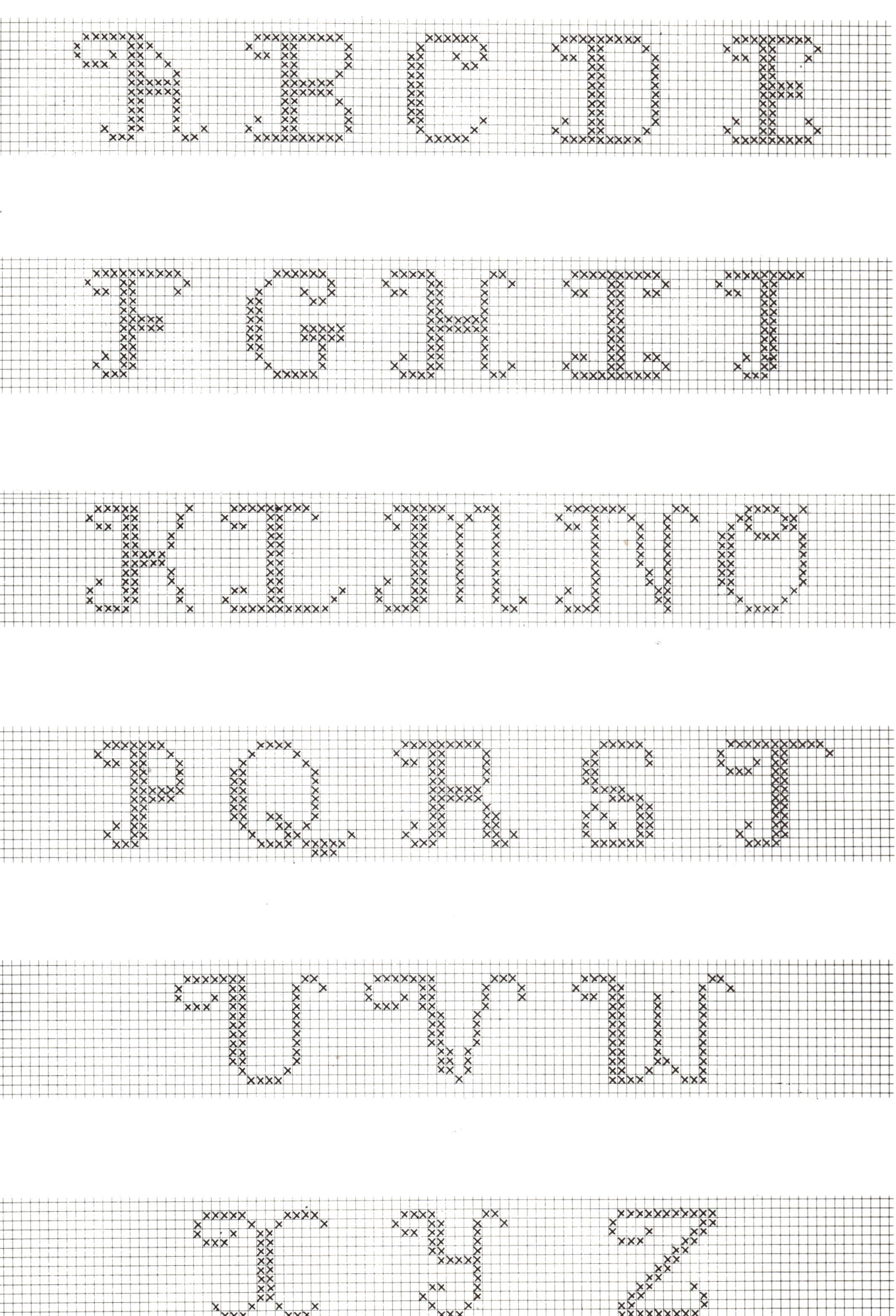

Block Alphabet
Shown for canvas size 12 and 14

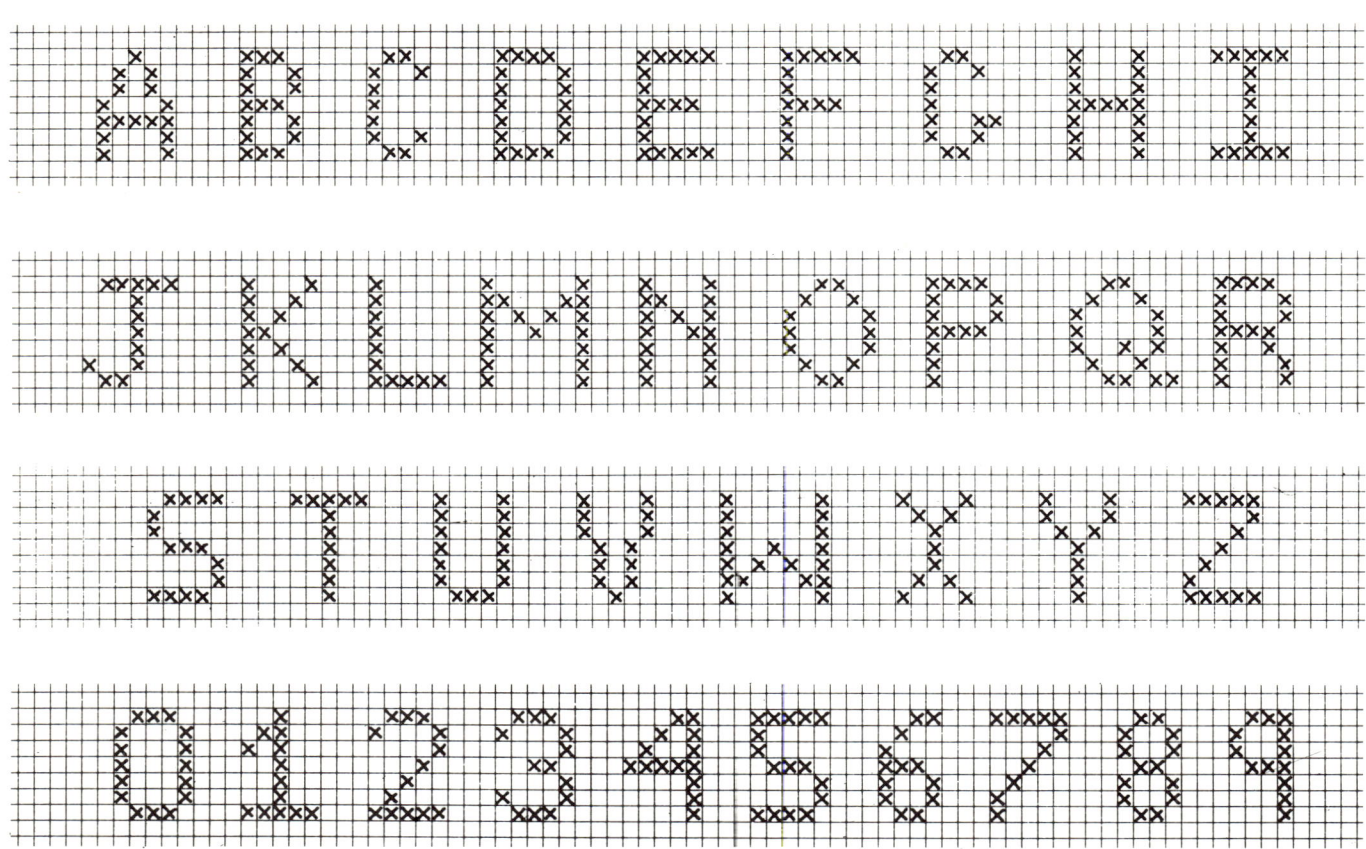

Nautical Signal Flags

Borders

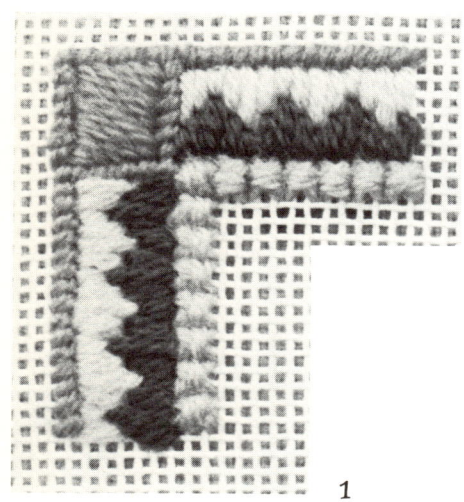

1

3

2

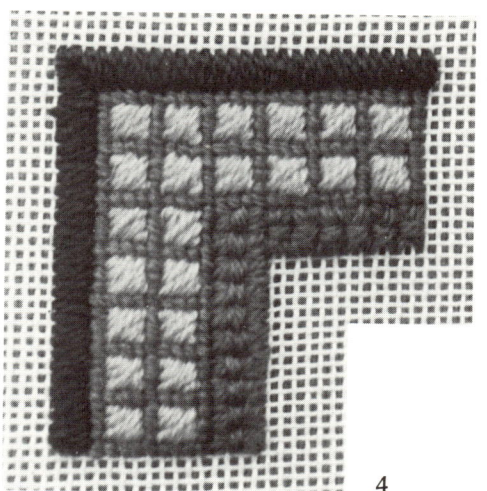

4

Ornamental Stitch Borders
These borders should be counted out on the canvas first and then the design should be centered within. Stitches are named from the inner edge out.

1. Oblong cross with back stitch, flame, large mosaic stitch in corner surrounded by continental stitch

2. Upright Gobelin, mosaic, long-armed cross stitch

3. Large cross stitch, Jacquard, cashmere, upright Gobelin

4. Tall oblong cross with back stitch, Scotch, upright Gobelin

Samplers

Mirror Frame
Connect the four sections of this design: see the completed sampler on the cover. (1) Mosaic stitch. (2) Parisian stitch. (3) Oblong cross with back stitch. (4) Double cross stitch. (5) Tent stitch. (6) Gobelin. (7) Cross stitch over four mesh. Sample on the cover. Canvas size 12–14

191

Pot of Flowers
(1) Milanese stitch. (2) Gobelin stitch. (3) Tent stitch. (4) Parisian stitch. (5) Double cross stitch. (6) Cashmere stitch. (7) Triangle stitch. (8) Oblique Slav stitch. (9) Cross stitch over four mesh. (10) Brick stitch (worked horizontally). (11) Oblong cross with a backstitch. (12) Fern stitch. (13) Jacquard stitch. (14) Brick stitch (worked vertically). (15) Monogram or date bordered by cross stitch over one mesh. (16) Turkey tufting. Canvas size 10

Tavern Sign
See page 194 for legend.

Butterfly
(1) Turkey tufting. (2) Oblong cross with backstitch. (3) Milanese stitch. (4) Gobelin stitch over four and over two threads. (5) Tent stitch. (6) Cashmere stitch. (7) Oblique Slav stitch. (8) Double cross stitch. (9) Jacquard stitch. (10) Parisian stitch. (11) Brick stitch (worked horizontally). (12) Triangle stitch. (13) Continental stitch. (14) Fern stitch. (15) Monogram or date surrounded by cross stitch over one mesh. (16) Butterfly outlined in cross stitch over four mesh. (17) Brick stitch (worked vertically). Sample on the cover. Canvas size 10

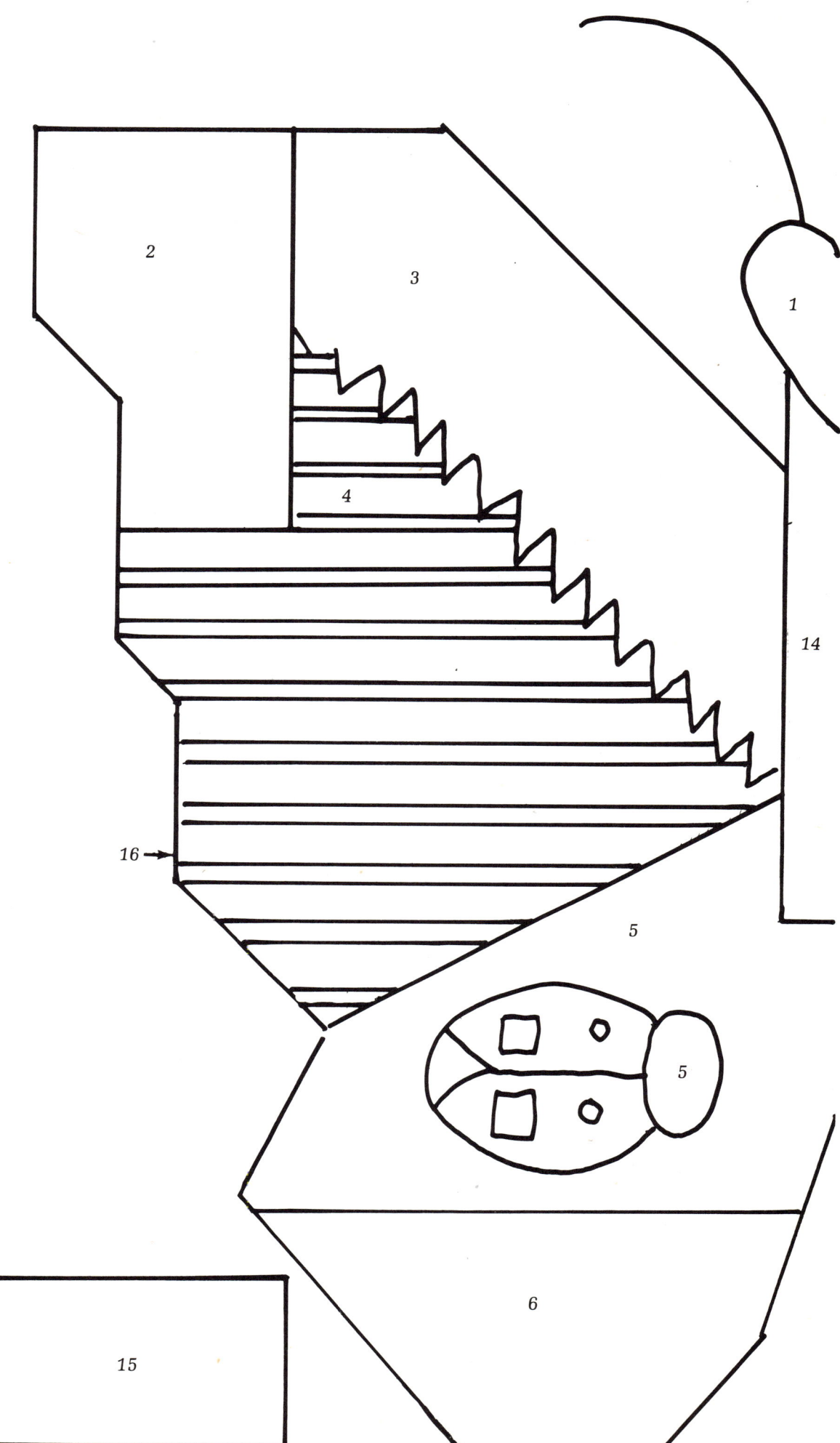

Tavern Sign (page 193)

Tavern Sign
Only nine stitches give this sampler its varied texture. It can also be worked plain. (1) Parisian stitch. (2) Bargello or flame stitch. (3) Leaf stitch. (4) Mosaic stitch. (5) Tent, embroidered over. (6) Tent stitch with enlarged mosaic "pillows." (7) Jacquard stitch. (8) Tent stitch. (9) Cross stitch over four mesh. Sample, page 202. Canvas size 12–14

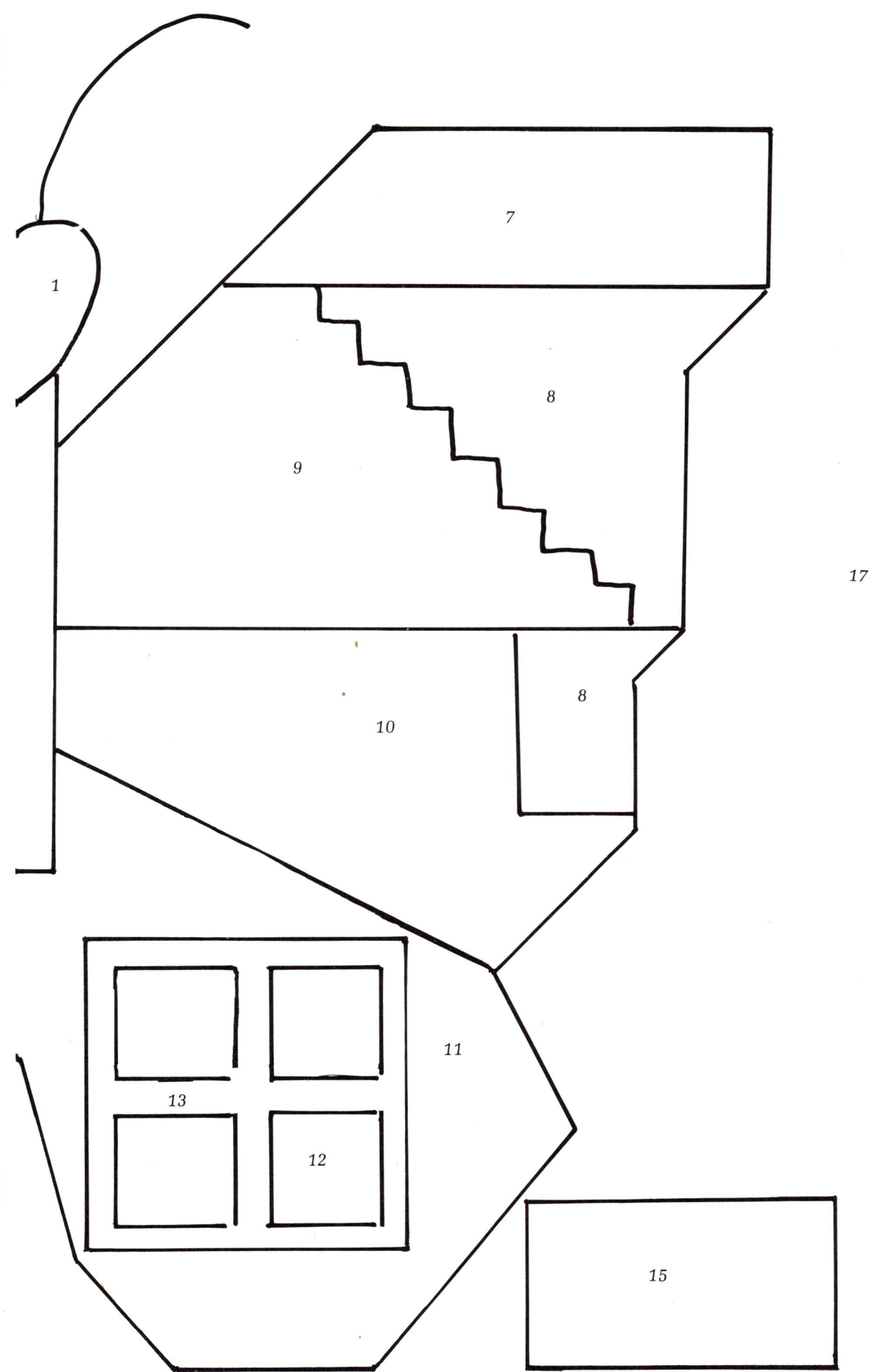

March Comes in Like a Lion
And goes out like a lamb. Odd-shaped pillow, or tea cozy. For some interesting effects try: Turkey tufting for the lion's mane and tail; French knots for the lamb's coat; bargello (flame stitch) for the church roof; alternating colors in double leviathan or double cross stitch for the checkered area and flowers; Parisian, Hungarian, or Milanese stitch for the diagonal line areas; Byzantine or Jacquard stitch for the zig-zag area; upright cross for the smoke, cloud, and center of sun; double cross stitch for the apples; and brick stitch for the background. Canvas size 12 (for tent stitch); 14 (for ornamental stitches)

Samples

Sunflowers worked by Joan Strathdee, Rye, New York. Design, pages 18-19. Shown in color on the cover.

Floral Motif worked by Harriett Bates, Jupiter, Florida. Design, page 23. The other side of this handbag is shown in color on the cover.

1880s Floral worked by Sharon Hiltz, Swarthmore, Pennsylvania. Design, page 26. Shown in color on the cover.

Sea Creatures worked by Gladys Reynolds, Tequesta, Florida. Design, page 104. The other side of this handbag is shown in color on the cover.

Christmas Ornaments worked by Joan Strathdee, Rye, New York. Designs, pages 144-47. Shown in color on the cover.

Cat worked by Martha Kennedy, Clarkston, Michigan. Design, pages 70-71.

Pennsylvania Dutch Floral motif worked by Ruth Foster, Scarsdale, New York. Design, page 175. Shown in color on the cover.

Red-winged Blackbird worked by Merrill Wilder and Blue Jay worked by Fessenden Wilder, Essex, Connecticut, Designs, pages 54, 55. Shown in color on the cover.

Butterfly worked by Janice Gablemann. Design, pages 194–95.

Tavern Sign worked by Janice Gablemann, Norfolk, Connecticut. Design, page 193.

Diagonal Geometric design worked by Jane Kennedy, Clarkston, Michigan. Design, page 117. Shown in color on the cover.

St. George and the Dragon worked by Martha R. Zimiles, Millerton, New York. Design, pages 92-93. Shown in color on the cover.

Medieval Castle worked by Sharon Hiltz, Swarthmore, Pennsylvania. Design, page 154. Shown in color on the cover.

Dolphins worked by Fessenden Wilder, Essex, Connecticut. Design, page 106.

Index of Designs

A
Accessory case, carnation, 17; Chinese flower, 29
Airplane, 122
Alphabet, fancy, 182, 183; block, 184; signal flag, 184
American eagle, 158-59
Anchor, 161
Apple, 109, 111, 112
Ark, 134-37
Artichoke, 112

B
Baby stroller, 126
Ball, 145, 163, 167
Banana, 108
Barn, 170, 196
Barnacle, 103
Barn swallow, 55
Baseball, 163, 167
Baseball bat, 167
Basket of flowers, 30
Bear, 80, 84, 135, 146
Beetle, 100
Beet, 113
Bell, 144
Bellflower, 21
Bell pull, flora, 14-15, 30-31
Belt, bug motif, 100; sportsman's, 167
Bermuda bag, 25
Bicycle, antique, 118
Bindweed, 34
Birthday cake, 115
Blackbird, red-winged, 54
Black-eyed Susan, 36
Block, children's toy, 174
Bluebird, 54
Blue jay, 55
Boar's head, 153
Boat, 127, 128, 167
Borders, 140-143, 176, 186, 187, 188-91
Bottle, 115
Bread, 114, 116, 117
Breakfast, 114
Broccoli, 112
Bug motifs, 69, 100
Buildings, 168-69, 170, 196, 197
Bus, 121
Butter, 117
Bunchberries, 21
Butterfly, 98, 99, 100, 101, 194-95

C
Cauliflower, 113
Candy cane, 147
Canoe, 16
Cardinal, 55, 57, 58
Cards, playing, 165
Carnation, 17
Carrot, 113
Car, 119, 120, 121, 123
Castle, 154
Cat, 70-71, 72-73, 74-75, 76; coat, 180-81; collar, 180
Caterpillar, 100
Checkbook cover, butterfly, 98
Cheese, 83
Cherries, 109
Chickadee, 54
Chicken, 69, 190
Chinese flower, 29
Chipmunk, 79
Christmas motifs, 144-47
Church kneeler, 139-43
Circus wagon, 124
Clover, red, 33
Clown, 124
Clutch bag, geometric design, 177
Coat, cat and dog, 180-81
Coat-of-arms, 150-51
Collars, cat, 180; dog, 179
Columbine, 35
Country store, 168-69
Cow, 170
Crab, 103, 105, 107, 137
Crêche, 147
Crochet hook case, 178-79
Crown, 153

D
Dachshund, 174
Daisy, 21, 36
Dandelion, 40
Deer, 85, 96-97
Dishes, 114
Diving mask, 167
Doberman pinscher, 87
Doe, 85
Dog, 87, 94-95, 130, 168-69, 174; coat, 180-81; collar, 179
Doll, 172-73
Dolphin, 106
Donkey, 136
Doorstop, cat, 70-71
Dove, 134-36
Dragon, 92-93
Duck decoy, 68
Dump truck, 120

E
Eagle, 158-59
Eggplant, 112
Egg, 69, 116
Elephant, 89, 124, 134-35
Evangelists, symbols, 140-43
Eyeglass case, bell flower, 21; bunch berries, 21; elephants, 89; hen and chicks, 69; paisley, 31; Pennsylvania Dutch, 175; shells, 107; wild rose, 29

F
Farm scene, 190
Fawn, 85
Feather, peacock, 62
Fire engine, 130-31
Fish, 102, 103, 104, 105, 135, 174
Fish hook, 167
Fleur-de-lys, 152, 153
Flippers, 167
Floral groupings, 12, 13, 14-15, 20, 22, 23, 24, 25, 26, 27, 30-31, 162-63, 176
Food, see individual items
Flag, American, 168
Fly, 100
Folk subjects, 91, 148, 168-69, 175
Football, 167
Fox hunt motif, 160
Frame, 176, 188-91
Frog, 83
Fruit motif, 108, 109, 112

G
Galleon, 127
Garlic, 110, 113
Geometric, abstract design, 177; flower, 14
George Washington, 91
Geranium, 162-63
Ginger man 147
Ginger maid, 147
Gingko leaf and fruit, 47
Giraffe, 136
Goldfinch, 55
Golf motifs, 163, 167
Gourds, 111
Grapes, 108, 132-33
Grasshopper, 100
Griffin, heraldic, 152-53

H
Handbag, 22-23, 27, 57, 104-5
Heart, 148-49
Helicopter, 122
Helmet, 150
Hen, 69
Heraldic shield, 150-51
Horse, 86, 91, 93, 124, 125, 134, 147, 161, 168, 169, 170
Horse chestnut nut and blossom, 50
Hunting motif, 94-95, 161

I
Indian, 169
Insect, 100
Iron stove, 171
Iris, 39

J
Jack of Spades, 165
Jam jar, 117
Jellyfish, 102, 104

K
Kangaroo, 84
Key, 154
Kingfisher, 58
Kneeler, church, 139–43
Knitting needle case, 178–79

L
Lady and hackney, 125
Ladybug, 100
Lamb, 137, 140–43, 178, 196
Lemon, 109
Leaf groupings, 42–43, 53
Lion, 152, 155, 157, 174, 197
Locomotive, 129
Locust leaf, blossom, and seed pod, 49
Luggage rack strap, floral, 30–31

M
Maple, leaf, 45; leaf, blossom, and seed pod, 48
March, month motif, 194–95
Matzoh cover, 132–33
Medieval lady with a cat, 90
Monkey, 97, 136–37
Mountain laurel, 41
Mouse, 81, 82, 83
Mushroom, 113
Musical notes, 164
Mythological animals, 67, 152–53, 155

N
Nativity scene, 147
Nautical, motifs, 167; signal flags, 184
Needle case, 178–79
Noah's Ark, 134–38

O
Oak leaf, acorn, and bract, 51
Octopus, 135–37
Onion, 110
Oil lamp, 171
Oriole, 60
Oranges and orange blossoms, 16
Owl, 64, 65, 66

P
Packard, 119
Paddle 164
Paisley, 31
Pansies, 19
Parrot, 56
Partridge, 63
Pennsylvania Dutch, abstract motif, 175; flowers, 175; heart and flowers, 148
Petunia, 28
Peacock feather, 62
Pear, 109, 111
Penguin, 68
People, 90, 91, 92, 124, 125, 134, 136
Pepper, 110, 111
Persian cat, 70
Pheasant, 59
Pig, 89
Pineapple, 108
Pine cone, 44
Pitcher, 115
Playing card suits, 165
Plum, 112
Pomegranate, 112
Poodle, 87
Pug, 87
Pumpkin, 111, 112

Q
Queen of Diamonds, 166

R
Raccoon, 88
Racing flag, 167
Racquet cover, squash, 166; tennis, 162–63
Rabbit, 70, 95, 134
Red clover, 33
Red-winged blackbird, 54
Rhinoceros, 137
Robin, 54
Rocking horse, 146
Rose, 20, 24, 29
Rooster, 135, 148–49, 193
Rudolph the Red-nosed Reindeer, 144
Rug, floral, 32–41; Noah's Ark, 134–37; tree-leaf, 46–51

S
Saint George and the Dragon, 92–93
Sampler, butterfly, 194–95; March, 194–95; mirror frame, 189–91; pot of flowers, 192; tavern sign, 193
Sandwich, 117
Santa Claus, 146
Saucepan, 115
Scarlet tanager, 58
Scissor case, 175
Sea anemone, 102
Seagull, 61
Seahorse, 105
Sea mussels, 103, 104
Seaweed, 103, 104, 105, 107
Sea urchin, 102
Sewing motifs, 178
Shell, 104, 105, 107, 187
Ship, 128
Ski cap, 167
Skis, 167
Snail, 105, 107
Snake, 134–35
Snowflake, 146
Snowman, 146
Snow scene, 147
Softball, 163
Spider and web, 98, 174
Sportsman's motifs, 167
Squash, 111
Squash racquet cover, 166
Squirrel, 77, 78, 134
Star, 158–59
Starfish, 107
Stove, 171
Strawberry, 82, 108
Sunflower, 18–19

T
Tabby cat, 76
Tavern sign, 190
Tea cozy, sleeping cat, 72–75
Tea pot, 115
Teddy bear, 146
Tennis racquet cover, 162–63
Terrier, 87
Thanksgiving turkey, 115
Tiger, 71, 135
Thistle, 44
Toad, 89
Toast, 114, 116, 117
Toaster cover, 116–17
Tower, 152–53
Toy, block, 174; doll, 172–73
Train, 129
Tray, frog, 83; mice, 83; pansiers, 19
Trillium, 37
Truck, 120

U
Unicorn, 155, 156

V
Vase of flowers, 13, 30–31, 148–49, 175, 192
Vegetable motifs, 110, 112, 113
Volkswagen, 121

W
Walnut leaf, nut, and bract, 46
Well, 170
Whale, 107
Wreath, Christmas, 145
Wren, 58